The Game
America Plays

Best
Wishes
Bill Plummer III

THE NATIONAL GOVERNING BODY
OF SOFTBALL

The Amateur Softball Association of America
2801 Northeast 50th Street
Oklahoma City, OK 73111-7203
Phone: (405) 424-5266
Fax: (405) 424-3855
Web site: asasoftball.com

The Game America Plays

Celebrating 75 Years of the Amateur Softball Association

Bill Plummer III
ASA Hall of Fame Manager
Oklahoma City

arnica
PUBLISHING, INC.
Portland, Oregon

Library of Congress Cataloging-in-Publication Data

Plummer, Bill, 1944-
  The game America plays : celebrating 75 years of the Amateur Softball Association / by Bill Plummer.
    p. cm.
  ISBN 978-0-9794771-7-1 (alk. paper)
  1. Softball-United States-History. 2. Amateur Softball Association of America-History. I. Title.

  GV863.A1P58 2008
  796.357'8-dc22

                        2008026851

The photo on the cover can be found on page 32. See page 157 for image credits and trademark information.

Senior Director of Project Development: Dick Owsiany
Cover and text design: Emily García

Editorial Team:
Gloria Martinez, editor-in-chief
Ehren Wells, editor
Jennie Chamberlin, copy editor
Rick Schafer, creative director
Aimee Genter, senior graphic designer
Michael Palodichuk, research assistant
Shannon Hunt, editorial assistant
Kristin Eberman, production assistant
Maria Sosnowski, indexer

Arnica Publishing, Inc.
3880 SE Eighth Ave, Suite 110
Portland, Oregon 97202
Phone: (503) 225-9900
Fax: (503) 225-9901
arnicacreative.com

Arnica books are available at special discounts when purchased in bulk for premiums and sales promotions, as well as for fund-raising or educational use.
Special editions or book excerption can also be created for specification. For details, contact the Sales Director at the address above.

This book is dedicated to William H. Plummer Jr. (deceased),
who instilled the love of sports to launch a career,
and to Anne D. Plummer,
who has been an inspiration not only to her family,
but to the many people that know her.

TABLE OF CONTENTS

FOREWORD

By Jennie Finch

This is a special year for the Amateur Softball Association, softball's national governing body. It's the 75th Anniversary of the founding of the organization (ASA), and helping to make it even more memorable is *The Game America Plays: Celebrating 75 Years of the Amateur Softball Association*. We are celebrating dedicated people and historical events that enabled the ASA, year-by-year, decade-by decade, to promote and to develop the game of softball in the United States.

It seems like only yesterday (it was actually 1989) that I was playing in the ASA National Championship in Northern California, where my 10-under team, the Cypress Curve, was defeated. Although feelings of disappointment overwhelmed me that day, I was determined more than ever to come back and win the national championship the next year at Chattanooga, Tennessee. We did, of course, and the thrill of that last out was so exciting as we ran towards each other, high-fiving and hugging, wearing smiles from ear-to-ear.

As I developed and matured on the field, I realized that softball was becoming an integral part of my life. I love the competiveness, the camaraderie, the game within a game, and the lifelong relationships that are developed. I will forever cherish the multiple weekends spent at softball fields and a special thank you to my Dad, who would come home after work and be my catcher. My family has always been there for me and I am forever grateful to all of them.

I followed the path that had been paved for me by some of the greatest softball players who've ever played the game, from Bertha Tickey and Joan Joyce, to Debbie Doom and Lisa Fernandez, pioneers who broke down barriers. It is a tremendous honor to carry on their torch. The Running Rebels and the Stratford Brakettes come to mind when I reflect on the foundation of ASA women's fast-pitch. Before them, the Jax Maids, the Fresno Rockets, Erv Lind Florists, the Phoenix Ramblers, and the Orange Lionettes were household names in women's fast-pitch.

In 1996, I vividly remember anxiously watching television and seeing Michele Smith and Dot Richardson take the field during the Olympics in Columbus, Georgia. What an amazing moment for USA Softball! The image of those athletes proudly taking their hard-earned place on the medal stand is something I will never forget. It inspired me to make the dream of wearing USA across my chest a reality.

A year later, as the ASA continued to foster my growth as an athlete, we were blessed to win the 18-under National Championship in Oklahoma City at the ASA Hall of Fame Stadium. As a member of the powerhouse Orange County Batbusters, we battled through the bracket before capturing the title against the Gordon Panthers. Little did I realize then what the ASA Hall of Fame Stadium would mean to me today.

Although there are other softball organizations, the caliber of play in the ASA is the best in the United States and the cream of the crop play ASA softball. Winning an ASA national championship is truly an honor.

The organization has developed the ASA Hall of Fame Stadium complex to be the mecca of softball in the United States and the environment and atmosphere are one-of-a-kind. Reaching the Hall of Fame Stadium is every softball player's dream because that is where champions are crowned.

The ASA has provided dreams not just for fast-pitch players, but for all disciplines of this sport including slow-pitch and modified pitch. This demonstrates how this sport can span an entire lifetime. I enjoy hearing stories from former teammates who keep their competiveness alive by playing in slow-pitch leagues and tournaments across the country. Softball is a sport for people of all ages, shapes, and sizes and the ASA has impacted the lives of millions of people who've enjoyed "The Game America Plays."

The words "dream and believe" are very close to my heart and I often express them in speeches or clinics because that is what the ASA has provided me and many others. For the past seventy-five years, as you'll read in this book, many people have dreamed and believed in ASA softball. If it wasn't for Leo Fischer and M.J. Pauley, the co-founders of the ASA, none of this would have happened.

PREFACE

My late father, William H. Plummer Jr., who loved sports despite having polio and rheumatic fever, was responsible for my getting involved in softball while growing up in Liverpool, a suburb of Syracuse, New York. At age fourteen, I attended a Syracuse Chiefs Triple A baseball game at MacArthur Stadium, fondly known as the North Side ball yard, with my dad, who was a big baseball fan. Before the game started, I noticed some non-baseball players warming up. One of them was in center field and was wearing a red, white, and blue uniform. I didn't know the player's name, but he got my attention quickly when he took one step and fired a softball windmill to home plate.

I thought, "Wow," wondering who that person was, and eventually I learned it was the legendary pitcher Eddie Feigner, of the King and His Court (in later years, we would get to know and even battle each other, becoming mutual friends along the way). That evening, Feigner and His Court played an exhibition game against the Syracuse Nationals basketball team. The Nats' Paul Seymour, who was a three-time NBA all-star, was also a standout hurler and, if I recall correctly, beat the King that evening. While it was a rare loss for the King and His Court, it was a "moment to remember" for me.

After watching that game, I started to follow softball, as well as other sports, and by the time I was nineteen I was playing city recreation fast-pitch. A year later, I enlisted in the Air Force and was fortunate enough to see some of the top men's players in the Air Force, including Chuck Epperson and Andy Lopez, while I covered the PACAF championship for Armed Forces Radio. I was stationed in Guam, which had an outstanding men's inter-service league, and covered the competition for the base newspaper, The

Tropic Topics, for which I also served as editor and sports editor.

As my career progressed, my interest in softball grew, and I wondered about possibly working in the game full-time. One day, I became involved with the New York State ASA when the commissioner at that time, Joe Costine, came into the *Syracuse Herald-Journal* sports department and asked me if I would like to get involved with this rule-making organization. "We need someone to do publicity for us," Costine said. I agreed without much coaxing. As I became more involved with the ASA, I thought about joining the national office in Oklahoma City. In 1979, I was offered the job, and since then I've enjoyed a journey that has had more highs than lows, with the writing of this book certainly being a high for me, as well as for the ASA.

Research is something I've always been interested in, and researching for this book has been a time-consuming, worthwhile effort that I hope ultimately will give others an "inside look" at an organization that has been tested more than once and stood the test of time. After seventy-five years, we're still ticking because of the love and passion of thousands of people who felt it was worth the effort and time to make the ASA the No. 1 softball organization in the United States.

Personally, my involvement has offered a lifetime of memories of "The Game America Plays," and has introduced me to some of the best and most dedicated people in the sport. I consider myself lucky to have worked with so many of them. It doesn't get any better than that. I hope you enjoy reading this book as much as I enjoyed helping to produce it with the Arnica team.

ACKNOWLEDGMENTS

It doesn't matter if you are playing softball or producing a book, you need a team of dedicated people to accomplish the goal. *The Game America Plays: Celebrating 75 years of the Amateur Softball Association* was fortunate in having a dedicated, professional bunch of people who gave "their all" from the first inning through the seventh inning to bring this book to fruition.

The author would like to thank Ron Radigonda, Mark Loehrs, Kelly McKeown, Craig Cress, Ronnie Isham, Steve Walker, Jennie Finch, Stephanie Henry, Julie Bartel, Ehren Wells, Dick Owsiany, Jess Heald, Hank Bassett, Dan Cohen, Ken Hackmeister, Gloria Martinez, Tom Mason, Bill Humphrey, Kevin Ryan, Al Maag, Donna Lamprecht, Carol Spanks, Marigold Hakanson, David Cunningham, Joe Phillips, Buck Johnson, Darby Veazey, Bobby Simpson, Bertha Tickey, Joan Joyce, Ken Rowe, Georgia Hill, Emily García, Jennie Chamberlin, Aimee Genter, Ross Hawkins, Rick Schafer, Melva Manning, Matt Gerber, Mattie Ivy, Rachael Turner, Shannon Hunt, Troy Turner, Diane Vines, and Michael Palodichuk, ASA Board of Directors Jack Aaron, G. Pat Adkison, Bill Cary, Andy Dooley, Amy Hillenbrand, JoAnn McGuire, John Miller, Stacey Nuveman, Bill Parks, Mick Renneisen, Joe Sproul, Michael White, E.T. Colvin, past president; Joey Rich, president and D. Stephen Monson, past president; and special thanks to the players, parents, fans, volunteers, ASA commissioners, Junior Olympic commissioners, umpires, player reps, managers, and scorekeepers.

Some people contributed more than others, of course, but that isn't the point. In playing softball different players contribute at different stages of the game to try to win the game. Such was the situation with this book. Some contributed in the first inning or the seventh inning, but they all contributed to producing the best book possible to mark the seventy-fifth anniversary of the Amateur Softball Association.

INTRODUCTION

The vicissitudes of modern sports still leave considerable room for doubt and arguments. In the case of softball, Bill Plummer III puts an end to both while introducing us to the real game that America plays and offering a stirring salute to the Amateur Softball Association of America (the governing body of organized softball in the United States) and to those who played a vital role in its seventy-five-year existence.

There is no person in the world more qualified than Bill to lead us on this odyssey, which begins with the organization's birth. His twenty-nine years of service to the ASA have given him an encyclopedic knowledge of softball, a knowledge that is exceeded only by his indisputable passion for the game.

Bill has come a long way since leaving his sports-writing job in Syracuse, New York, to assume the far-ranging managerial duties at the Oklahoma City-based ASA. He has served as the association's historian, trade show manager, director of public relations, and author of many softball periodicals. He served as an information specialist in Guam and on bases in the U.S. while serving in the U.S. Air Force. His work earned him the prestigious Ernie Pyle Scholarship at Indiana University, where he graduated with other honors. His resumé reveals many other communications awards, including citations from the NCAA Women's College Softball World Series, Olympic Festivals, the 1996 Atlanta Olympic Games, and induction into the ASA Hall of Fame and the ASA Halls of Fame in both New York and Indiana. Now he's the director of the ASA Hall of Fame.

Plummer will show you that the ASA's seventy-five-year story is more than just a sport; it's a story that deserves a special place in American history. The organization is an offspring of a grieving yet hard-working American society battling the Great Depression. The game the organization promotes brought joy to thousands who didn't know where their next meal was coming from. It brought happiness to the rich and poor alike, regardless of race or of social standing, and provided a weary society a chance to indulge in a simple fun-filled game.

Plummer will tell you about the tremendous successes of four strong-willed men who have each served as executive directors and led the ASA ship through the stormy seas of time, bringing the game of softball from middle America's vacant barnyards and empty fields to servicemen abroad on the battlefields of war and ultimately to the world on center stage of the Olympic Games. Since its inception, the ASA has organized softball play that has become a lovable attraction to millions of participants. With more than 30,000 players annually earning a spot in one of the more than 100 ASA National Championship tournaments, one must give an appreciative nod to the organization for a job well done.

Throughout his career with the ASA, Plummer has been an eyewitness to the record-setting performances of many of the softball heroes and heroines who have cascaded down the corridors of time. Yet he will be the first to tell you that none of these records is carved in stone. Some records are equaled and some are smashed by the battering ram of the young superstars of recent years. Few will survive the test of time. However fleeting these great players may seem, Plummer won't allow you to forget any of them, even if their names seem to have been lost in the dust of the historic road to softball immortality. We welcome you to sit back and enjoy the wonderful world of Bill Plummer III and the ASA.

Let the odyssey begin.

TIMELINE

1933

Leo Fischer and M.J. Pauley host a softball tournament in conjunction with the World's Fair, from which the Amateur Softball Association of America (ASA) emerges.

1934

The national champions are the Ke-Nash-A Motormakers of Kenosha, Wisconsin in the men's division, and Hart Motors of Chicago in the women's division. The International Joint Rules Committee on Softball holds its first meeting.

1936

The ASA affiliates with the Amateur Athletic Union (AAU). Four sectional vice-presidents are elected to assist Leo Fischer and M.J. Pauley run the ASA.

1937

The ASA prints *SoftBalls and Strikes*, a thirty-two-page publication that highlights the national championship. The publication is discontinued in 1942, but is revitalized in 1947 as the present-day namesake, *Balls and Strikes*.
National championships in Chicago are carried across the airwaves, marking softball's first play-by-play radio broadcast.

1938

A Board of Governors is created to assist commissioners in running the ASA.

1942

Due to war-time restrictions on travel, the women's national championship is reduced to ten teams. The small field prompts the use of the double-elimination system, and it proves so successful that format is still used today in championship play.

1948

The ASA Council votes to hold the 1949 men's and women's national championships at separate sites—the first time the events will not be held at the same venue.

1950

Standard uniforms are adopted for ASA umpires.
First season for the ASA's first female umpire, Madeline Lorton, from the Bronx, New York. She umpires thirty-five games in her first season.

1951

The NCAA reaffirms recognition of the ASA as sole governing body of amateur softball.

Lou Hamilton becomes the ASA's first female commissioner.

As a tribute to the sport, National Softball Week is initiated, from July 22–28.

1953

The First National Umpire Interpretations Clinic is held from March 27–29 in New York City.

Slow-Pitch is added to the ASA National Championship Program.

1955

U.S. President Dwight Eisenhower recognizes National Softball Week.

1956

Regional Umpire clinics are held for the first time.

1957

The ASA National Softball Hall of Fame is established. Harold "Shifty" Gears of Rochester, NY, is the first inductee. He is joined by fellow fast-pitch players Marie Wadlow, Sam Elliott and Amelita Peralta May Shelton.

Full-scale youth program is adopted.

The ASA celebrates its silver anniversary.

1958

Official rules are recodified for the first time.

1959

Umpires are included under the ASA Insurance program. The ASA garners its first national TV exposure, as NBC carries coast-to-coast finals of the women's national tournament.

John Nagy, metro Cleveland commissioner, plans to introduce a "mixed couples" league. The league will be designed to encourage co-ed participation.

1965

Oklahoma City, Oklahoma, is announced as the new ASA headquarters.

Melbourne, Australia, hosts the first ISF Women's World Fast-Pitch Championship, with the hosts winning the gold. The U.S. finishes second.

1966	The first ISF Men's World Fast-Pitch Championship is held in Mexico City, and the United States wins the title. The first umpire instructional film is produced.
1967	Softball is accepted as a demonstration sport in the Pan-American Games, being held in Winnipeg, Manitoba, Canada. The ASA National Umpire Staff is founded.
1970	On December 19, ground is broken for construction of a new ASA headquarters building and National Softball Hall of Fame in Oklahoma City. Leo Fischer, one of the founders of ASA, dies in Chicago.
1971	The first *ASA Case Book* for umpires is printed.
1972	An Umpire-in-Chief (UIC) is named for each state and metro association. Construction on the new ASA headquarters and National Softball Hall of Fame is completed.
1973	The ASA National Softball Hall of Fame is officially dedicated on May 26. The first state and metro UIC clinics are held. Slow-pitch players are now eligible for Hall of Fame Induction.
1974	ASA team registration breaks the 50,000 barrier for a season. Junior Girls 18-under and 16-under fast-pitch tournaments are added to national tournament programs.
1975	The first modified pitch national tournament is held, with Port Huron, Michigan, hosting. 75,000 teams register for the year.
1976	The ASA Hall of Honor is established to recognize non-players who have contributed to the sport.

1977
In first overall change since 1950, a revamped ASA code is adopted. The ASA is recognized as a Class A member of the United States Olympic Committee (USOC), due to softball being added to the program of the Pan American Games.

1978
The USOC names the ASA the National Governing Body of Softball. Team registration eclipses 100,000 for the season.
Softball is included in the first National Sports Festival, which is held in Colorado Springs.
Player representatives are established.

1979
Softball makes its debut in the Pan-American Games. The U.S. wins the women's division and takes silver in the men's competition.
For the first time, the ASA registers more than 100,000 adult teams in a season.
The "Play at Home" sculpture, by Leonard McMurry, is dedicated June 23 outside the ASA National Hall of Fame.

1981
The first ISF World Youth Fast-Pitch Championships are held. Edmondton, Alberta, Canada hosts the event, and the U.S. wins silver in both the boys' and girls' divisions.
The Super Division is started for the top men's slow-pitch teams.

1982
The ASA's youth program is officially designated as Junior Olympic (JO) Softball.
Plans are announced that the ASA will build a Hall of Fame Stadium on the grounds of the National Office complex in Oklahoma City.
The ASA celebrates its golden anniversary.

1985
Ground is broken for construction of the ASA Hall of Fame Stadium. The project is completed in 1987.

1987
Softball's centennial year is celebrated with various events, including a torch run from Chicago, the birthplace of softball, to Oklahoma City.

1990	The ASA Hall of Fame Stadium hosts its first NCAA Women's College World Series.
1991	On June 13, the International Olympic Committee (IOC) announces that women's fast-pitch softball will be an official sport on the program of the 1996 Olympic Games in Atlanta. For the first time, JO registration tops 50,000 teams in a season.
1993	A seven-member Olympic Team Selection Committee is selected.
1994	The JO Gold Program is initiated, providing the highest level of competition for girls 18-and-under.
1995	A fifteen-player Olympic team roster is named.
1996	The USA women win the first Olympic gold medal for softball.
1997	The ASA ventures into cyberspace, launching its first Web site.
1999	Plans are finalized to make the ARCO Olympic Training Center the official training site of the USA Softball National Team program. Construction of a playing field, practice infield, batting cages and pitching areas is completed the next year.
2000	The U.S. successfully defends its Olympic gold medal. After years of research, the ASA begins enacting its Bat Testing and Certification Program.
2001	The first USA Softball Hooters National Championship Series is played, hosted by the ASA Hall of Fame Stadium.
2004	The U.S. Women's National team becomes a three-time Gold Medalist with an unprecedented 9–0 record.

2005   The ASA hosts its first-ever World Cup featuring the top women's national teams from across the World. Japan shocks the United States by winning the inaugural event.

2006   Oklahoma City plays host to the 18-under Gold National Championship and is televised on the ESPN networks.

2008   The ASA celebrates its 75th anniversary.

The Game
America Plays

CHAPTER I

1930s

THE BEGINNING

The summer of 1933 was anything but typical. The United States was in the midst of the Great Depression (1929-1939), and it wasn't a good time to launch a new business, let alone a national sports organization. The collective heartbeat of America's people wasn't a strong one. They had a look of despair and hopelessness in their eyes—sort of a faraway look. They didn't know from one day to the next where they were headed, and their sense of hope and optimism had turned to despair and uncertainty. The land of opportunity was now the land of desperation. But as Frederick Wilcox once said, "Progress always involves risk; you can't steal second base and keep your foot on first base."

Remarkably, despite the long odds of success, Leo Fischer and Maurice (Mike) J. Pauley were more than willing to step out of the bread lines and up to the plate for a dream they felt was worth the risk. That leap of faith, which ultimately became the Amateur Softball Association, will celebrate its seventy-fifth anniversary in 2008.

Although Fischer and Pauley are credited with founding the ASA, it was George Hancock, a reporter for the Chicago Board of Trade, who invented the game of softball, from inside the Farragut Boat House in Chicago in 1887. During the '20s and '30s, the sport had as many as twenty-two different names (such as Kitten Ball, Playground Ball, Night Ball, Army Ball, and Mush Ball) and rules depended on where in the United States teams lived and played. As you can imagine, this disparity led to a sea of confusion and unpredictability as a baseball-crazy nation tried to get behind the concept. Despite the tremendous interest it had created in certain parts of the country, baseball's "little sister sport" was going nowhere fast.

Softball found new direction, however, when Fischer, assistant sports editor for the *Chicago American*, and Pauley, a sports entrepreneur, accepted an invitation from the organizers of the 1933 Chicago World's Fair to stage a softball tournament, which was held September 2-9. Wrote Fischer in his book, *Winning Softball*, "M.J. Pauley and I were asked to conduct it, because of our success with a local tournament in Chicago in which more than 1,000 teams participated.

"Teams were brought in from a dozen states—and then the trouble began. Each had its own idea on how the game should be played. Some used 40-foot baselines. Others

From top: Leo Fischer and M.J. Pauley, the founders of the ASA. **Facing page:** the Farragut Boat House in Chicago where softball was invented on Thanksgiving Day, 1887.

Heavy rains forced teams to practice on a roof top during the 1935 ASA National Championship in Chicago.

had 70-foot intervals between the bags. Some permitted base-stealing. Others didn't. Three or four different sizes of balls were in use. There was only one thing to do. We wrote an arbitrary set of rules and turned the teams loose on a diamond built under one of the huge sky-ride towers which dominated the Chicago fair." In those first championships, teams used a fourteen-inch ball, and games other than the semis and finals were seven-innings long.

Because softball was still relatively unknown at the time, the fair organizers were less than optimistic about the idea, but in August, Pauley and Fischer got the green light. The organizers gave them $500 and ten days to pull everything together. "This looked like a whale of a job and would not have been

successful if it not been for the efforts of Leo Fischer," wrote Pauley in the *Worth Book of Softball*. "He wrote stories tirelessly and besieged wire services with articles, which they took only as a favor to him and not because they thought that softball deserved the time and money it required to send the stories out.

"We climbed into the car and every state we heard of where any sort of a softball tournament was being conducted, the winning team was invited to this first national softball championship event. The meet attracted [a grand total of fifty-five teams]. They came from Colorado, Louisiana, Georgia, Connecticut, Kentucky, Illinois, Indiana and nine other states. We had a cross-section of the nation represented."

Continued on page 5

The Great Depression

To understand just how monumental it was for Fischer and Pauley to have started the ASA when they did, it's important to look at the overall financial climate of the Great Depression. As with today, the country's economic well-being had a great influence on the citizens' happiness and motivation. The Depression was a time when families struggled to live above the poverty line. Most people's energies were spent finding work and putting food on the table, yet Pauley and Fischer found the energy to pioneer and promote a sports organization.

The stock market crash on October 29, 1929, was a harbinger of things to come. A record 16,410,030 shares were traded on Black Tuesday, as it is commonly referred to, and by December 1 of that year, stocks had dropped in value by $26 million as panic engulfed the stock exchange—all this taking place at a precipitous rate, with no computers to record the deals.

In the following year, sixty percent of the U.S. had incomes of less than $2,000, and as many as 1,300 banks failed. The stock market crash had lingering effects, too, because even two-and-a-half years later, U.S. industry operated at less than half its maximum 1929 volume.

Milton Friedman, in *A Monetary History of the United States, 1867 – 1960*, wrote that the downturn in the economy starting with the stock mark crash would have been just another recession. In general, he states the problem was that some bank failures produced widespread runs on banks. He claims that if the Federal Reserve had acted by providing emergency lending to these key banks or simply bought government bonds on the open market to provide liquidity and increase the quality of money after the key banks fell, subsequent bank failures would have been prevented, and the money supply would not have fallen so quickly, or to the extent that it did.

Although President Herbert Hoover did his part to stem the tide of economic woes by reducing his personal salary by 20 percent, the economic downturn continued. By 1932, 13 million people were unemployed and wages were 60 percent less than in 1929.

The American people, having become increasingly dissatisfied with President Hoover, elected Franklin D. Roosevelt to succeed him. Roosevelt was inaugurated on March 4, 1933, and rapidly put into place his New Deal, which was an active, diverse, and innovative program of economic recovery. When FDR took over, the banking system had collapsed, and nearly 25 percent of the labor force was unemployed. Factories were shut down, many homes and farms were foreclosed, mills and mines were abandoned, and people found out the real meaning of being hungry.

What made this Depression worse than the periodic depressions America had encountered in the past was that the culture had changed. In the past, many people lived on farms and could produce what they needed. That wasn't the case because, according to Kenneth C. Davis, the "world economy had been revolutionized. This was an urbanized, mechanized America in which millions were suddenly unemployed with no farms to go home to."

Although the U.S. finally overcame the Depression, its effects lingered into the early 1940s. The Great Depression, however, finally came to an end when the U.S. entered World War II. By 1945, 17 million had entered the service, and unemployment almost disappeared. Only five years earlier (1940) the number of unemployed was 8,120,000 out of a total population of 132,122,000. With so many people available to work at a time when the country really needed them, a new market of civilian jobs in the defense and war industries was created, eventually helping to pull the U.S. out of the Great Depression.

M.J. Pauley
A Founding Father

· · · · · · · · · · · · · · · · ·

For whatever reason, M.J. Pauley was often called Mike or M.J. Mike, however, wasn't his real name. "Maurice was his real name," said his daughter-in-law, Mary Juanita Pauley. "Even his own sons didn't know his real name." Juanita found this out from Mike Pauley's wife, Genevine.

Juanita married the Pauleys' oldest son, Robert, in 1947. They lived in St. Petersburg, Florida with M.J. and Genevine while Robert attended college. Juanita and Robert would often help M.J. with ASA mailings from the Municipal Pier in St. Petersburg, the ASA's winter home from November to May. Robert went on to become a lawyer and a county court judge before passing away from lung cancer in 1963 at age thirty-six, leaving Juanita alone to care for their four children, two boys and two girls. Juanita was remarried in 1968 to James Cowan, who passed away in 2003.

Juanita, who celebrated her eighty-first birthday in 2008, lives in Newport Richey, Florida, just north of St. Petersburg. "He ate, drank and slept softball," said Juanita of Pauley. "His heart was in it." Because of Pauley's early work, the ASA continued to flourish and grow, even as it faced the growing pains and lack of cash flow typical of any new organization.

M.J. Pauley served the ASA for sixteen years, eventually resigning as executive secretary in 1949, just prior to the Annual Meeting in Chicago. At that time, Byron Eugene Martin, former New Jersey Commissioner and Eastern V.P., was asked to step in as Pauley's successor. Martin's career began in 1946, after the ASA's 1945 decision in New York to split the secretary-treasurer post into two positions; Martin was asked to fill the role of treasurer. Up to that time, Pauley had served a dual role as secretary-treasurer. Although Pauley didn't attend the meeting, he agreed with the decision. Martin was hired as national treasurer in 1946, with a starting salary of $1000, which the ASA increased to $1500 in 1947. That same year, they increased Pauley's salary as secretary to $7800.

Pauley passed away in September of 1952, three years after resigning from his position with ASA. His relatives are proud of his accomplishments in softball, especially his co-founding of the ASA with Leo Fischer. They should be proud, as should be the millions of people who have been involved with the ASA since 1933. The two men persevered when it would have been just as easy to give up the dream. Fortunately, they didn't, and the world of ASA softball is better because of it.

Left: M.J. Pauley (center) at the office before the 1941 ASA National Championship in Detroit. **Right:** presentation of 1941 Pepsi-Cola World Championship trophy to the Bendix Brakes of South Bend, IN Pictured are (from left to right) Jack Ledden, ASA Indiana commissioner; M.J. Pauley, ASA executive secretary; Ted Andrews, manager of the Bendix Brakes; and Wilbur E. Landis Jr., president of the ASA.

Fischer and Pauley gave no promise of travel money, room, or board, as there wasn't so much as a dime left in the $500 budget, spent mainly on promotion, to purchase trophies. Yet fifty-five teams came—some by car, either driving or hitchhiking, and even some by bicycle. As for the amenities, teams slept in tents and "feasted" on bologna and bread. "It is the largest and most comprehensive tournament ever staged in the sport which has swept the county like wildfire," reported the *Chicago American*. "Fifty title winners from Colorado to New Jersey and from Minnesota to Florida have sent their winners. The diamond is located on Northerly Island, near the east town of the Sky Ride and bleacher space is available for thousands of spectators."

With free admission and unemployment at an all-time high, (growing to more than five million in 1930 and up to thirteen million in 1932), there were many people with plenty of time to attend the event. In fact, more than 350,000 people attended, including 70,000 who attended the first round of the single-elimination event.

"We just didn't know what we had a hold of back there in 1933," Fischer wrote. "We liked the game, wanted to popularize it and keep it alive. We never thought it would grow into a tremendous giant overnight. Girls had taken up play at almost the same time as did men. And they played it well. This was so because many had participated in playground ball during earlier years on the recreation grounds. When we sketched out the rules for the men's 'world series' of 1933 we decided to include one for girls' teams as well. We didn't think it would go very well, but we didn't want to slight the ladies. They could have their chance, if they wanted it. It developed that they wanted it, and the play for the ladies' championship game of 1933 really featured our program."

When the dust settled at the tournament's end, Chicago's Great Northern

Laundry had prevailed in the women's division, winning 18-3, and the Coon Rosen-led J.L. Friedman Boosters had won the men's division, beating Briggs Body Works, 5-1. In all, the event was viewed as a tremendous success on the playing field, convincing Fischer and Pauley more than ever that America needed a national softball organization. So they forged ahead, setting up an office in the Morrison Hotel in Chicago. Fischer served as president without a salary, and Pauley served as executive secretary with a full-time salary of $2600, despite the fact that the organization had no funds. Thus together Leo Fischer and M.J. Pauley had laid the foundation, from which would emerge softball's national governing body—the Amateur Softball Association.

Because they didn't have any money, Fischer and Pauley's first order of business was to look to other organizations for support. The Athletic Institute and the *Chicago American* agreed to help with the finances, and this allowed the two to form associations and appoint commissioners nationwide. The Athletic Institute contributed $5,200 to the ASA through 1938, financing among other things some of the trips Pauley and Fischer made throughout the United States. The *Chicago American* paid the utility bills, including lights and telephone.

1933 was a big year for softball's new governing body. "The tournament was successful enough, but it was also a turning point in the game of softball," wrote Fischer in *Winning Softball*. "It brought home the need for uniformity in rules." To address that need, the organization held its first rules meeting at Chicago's Hotel Sherman. That meeting led to the formation of the International Joint Rules Committee on Softball (IJRCS). Many will recognize that committee, which helped to alleviate the confusion of 1933.

Continued on page 11

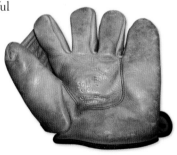

From top: softball glove from the 1930s; glove from the late 1930s; glove from the late 1930s; glove from the early 1940s.

Following the Rules

Concerning rule changes, softball evolved through four stages: the birth of indoor baseball, 1887; the beginning of playground baseball in 1908; the organization of the NAPBA (National Amateur Playground Ball Association); and, finally, the establishment of the ASA in 1933. Playground ball was the forerunner of softball. Also, at one time there were twenty-two different names tied to softball, according to Walter Hakanson, former ASA president and commissioner (source: *Balls and Strikes*, February 15, 1951).

The formation of the ASA and the International Joint Rules Committee of Softball (IJRCS) gave softball what it had lacked since its invention in 1887—stability. The development of the ASA's U.S. state and metro associations gave the sport a solid organization, while the IJRCS allowed the participants to play under a consistent set of rules that the ASA administered and standardized. Through the years, the IJRCS discussed numerous rule changes, passing rules they felt were in the best interest of the game.

The committee was open to discussing and hearing different rules from "all who are interested in the matter of better rules," and to studying the rules to improve the game where possible. The rules they passed in many cases helped to increase offense in the game or to make softball more interesting for fans or safer for the participants. They were also mainly for fast-pitch, although some applied to slow-pitch, as this was the method of play in the first ASA National Championship at the World's Fair in Chicago. The number of slow-pitch rule changes was minimal in the beginning compared to the number for fast-pitch. But as slow-pitch outgrew fast-pitch in the number of teams participating, the ASA developed more rules for slow-pitch. Though research and development wasn't pursued as intensely or to the degree it is today, softball continued to increase in popularity, and the ASA continued adding new rules from as few as two to as many as twenty new rules per year.

The tenth player rule was removed in 1947. Once softball moved outdoors, ten players per team was the norm. There was a first baseman, second baseman, third baseman, right shortstop, left shortstop, left fielder, center fielder, right fielder, pitcher, and a catcher.

With the change in rules came changes in terminology, as exemplified in this excerpt by Mary Littlewood, in *The Path to the Gold: An Historical Look at Women's Fastpitch in the United States*: "a 'fairly delivered ball' in 1935 is now called a strike; an 'unfairly delivered' ball is a ball; the 'batsman' has become known as the batter; the 'coacher' is either the first-base coach or third-base coach; and a 'bunt hit ball' is now called a bunt."

The International Joint Rules Committee on Softball held its first meeting at the Hotel Sherman in Chicago from January 20 to 22, 1934. Delegates from 37 states attended.

Pitching: Getting More Offense in the Game

As softball went from indoors to outdoors, the pitchers gradually developed their pitching styles to dominate the game, earning numerous double-digit strikeout totals per game.

Officials and players alike, particularly in men's softball, debated on how to get more offense into the

Lewis Rober Sr., a fire lieutenant, called the version of softball he invented in 1895 "Kitten Ball." His original stitching board, pictured above, is on display in the ASA Hall of Fame.

game, primarily by increasing the distance between the pitcher's box and home plate. Some people wanted the pitching distance moved to forty-five feet, while others wanted it left unchanged at forty feet. After meeting at the Morrison Hotel in Chicago in September of 1939, the International Joint Rules Committee found a compromise and voted that the new pitching distance be set at forty-three feet for men's softball but left unchanged at thirty-five feet for women's softball.

During the same meeting, the committee also passed a rule that allowed batters in both men's and women's leagues to try to get to first base when the catcher failed to catch a third-strike pitch. And the committee further extended the pitching rule by requiring that the pitcher keep both feet on the pitcher's plate for at least one second before the wind-up. This rule prevented pitchers from walking into the pitcher's box before pitching, a movement that more

often than not caught batters off guard. In addition to initiating these rule changes, the committee took time to consider but ultimately reject twelve others that ASA members had either suggested or formally introduced.

Even with the new rules, the pitchers still dominated in fast-pitch, with the pitching distance for women changed to thirty-five feet in 1946, to thirty-eight feet in 1952, forty feet in 1965 and forty-three feet in 2000 (Women's Major) and 2001 (Women's fast-pitch). The men's distance went from thirty-seven feet, eight and a half inches, to forty feet in 1936, to forty-three feet in 1940, and finally to forty-six feet in 1950. The IJRCS approved the forty-six-foot distance at a meeting on September 7, 1949, in Little Rock. They passed the vote after considerable discussion, as there were three committee members opposed to the three-foot increase.

One such opponent, Clarence E. Brewer, chairman of the committee, said, "It was my belief,

Clarence E. Brewer, first chairman of the IJRCS.

and still is after talking with umpires over the country, that the batters are always catching up with the fast ball pitchers and always take a short chop at the ball instead of a full swing. The cause of the large number of strikeouts is the curve or the 'break' which pitchers are able to put on the pitch. My contention was that if the pitcher's distance was moved back it would enable the pitcher to put a greater curve or break on the ball as it would travel a longer distance. Also, by increasing the pitching distance the pitcher was always pretty close to second base and always had to be alert and duck a throw from home to second base and he always will have to watch out for any throws from shortstop to first base."

The pitching rules were the most controversial and difficult to interpret, according to Daniel Leviton in his thesis, *The Evolution of the Rules of Softball* (1956). One of the important rule changes involving pitching came in 1932, when the pitcher was prohibited from striking his side with his forearm while delivering the ball. There was reason to believe that the pitcher, by striking his side with his pitching arm during the delivery, increased the amount of spin on the ball, thus increasing the amount of "break" on the ball. The pitcher, up to the 1920s, was not a highly skilled performer and, according to Leviton, had not developed either blinding speed or a deceptive variety of curves and junk. For a great many years, the pitcher

Pitcher and manager Frank Rorek warms up prior to a game. He is shown here wearing the solid dark "undertaker" uniform required for pitchers by a rule adopted in 1939.

was prohibited from curving the ball. His main function was to "get the ball over the plate and let them hit it." Since the first, pitchers in playground ball were allowed to curve the ball, but it was not until the late 1920s that the game became so competitive on a national scale that the pitcher began to evolve into the specialist he (or she) is today.

The "undertaker" rule required the pitcher to wear a darker uniform than the rest of the team because it was believed that it made the ball easier for the batter to see. In 1939, the pitcher wore a totally solid-dark uniform. This rule was changed in 1940, but by 1948 there was no mention of a specific type of uniform for the pitcher, and consequently he was allowed to wear the same uniform as the rest of the team. Lengthening the pitching distance gave the batter a longer look at the ball, which may have helped to eliminate the need for the "undertaker" uniform look of the pitchers, who were obviously the center of focus on the diamond; and it made more sense to have the pitcher dress like the rest of the team. In all, it took nine years for opponents to get this rule out.

In 1970, the ASA rescinded its previous decision to increase the base distance to sixty-five feet, and approved the distance at sixty feet. In 1973, they added a circle around the pitcher's mound and established the penalty of a ball put on the batter if the pitcher exceeded the limit of five warm-up pitches, thus helping to speed up the game. Gradually, by the early 1990s, they moved the base distance to sixty-five feet and the pitching distance to fifty-five feet (slow-pitch).

As slow-pitch emerged as the people's sport, combined with the upgrades in technology, the fence distance, pitching distance, and base distance all changed gradually. In the early days of slow-pitch championship play, men's teams played a "Punch-and-Judy" version, punching the ball into the gaps, with minimal home runs and low-scoring games. But homers and higher scores became more frequent as the equipment got better and the players went to working out almost year around.

Seven Innings

A regulation softball game is seven innings. Why not nine innings? Clarence E. Brewer, chairman of the International Joint Rules Committee on Softball, offered an explanation. As quoted in Evolution of the Rules of Softball by Daniel Leviton, 1956, Brewer said, "Seven innings was chosen as the official length of the game at the very beginning of the rise in popularity of the game. The game started out as a game played largely on playgrounds and it was desirable to play one or two games after dinner, and it was necessary to make the game seven innings, which could be played in an hour or an hour and a half. Furthermore, the game became popular before any daylight saving time was in effect. It is singular that only a few requests have even been made to make the official game a nine inning game."

Moving Toward Uniformity

Hank Bassett, a member of the ASA National Softball Hall of Fame and a former manager, said the emergence of the Internet helped the sport take off. "Through the Internet, players became more aware of training and getting into shape, plus bats (metal bat was approved in 1970) and balls (what's legal and what's illegal)," Bassett said. Before the Internet, players had to rely on what they heard from other players and teams and what they might read in a magazine or a local newspaper about some phase of softball. Now, if they want to know something about softball they get online and go to a search engine to get the information they need. Hall-of-Famer Carol Spanks said, "Technology, in all its forms, has provided much more information to the coaches and players which, in turn, have advantaged them in increasing their skill levels and knowledge of the game."

Although Spanks was retired as a player when many of the rule changes happened, she saw the changes as a college coach and in the summer she had an ASA major women's fast-pitch team with fellow Hall-of-Famer Shirley Topley, who in her own right was an outstanding player and coach. Because of the livelier balls and bats, there was much more offense in the game than in the past, and the increased pitching distance allowed the players more time to see the ball better. "More opportunities are presented for even increasing the offense more with the addition of the designated player rules," said Spanks. "There are just a lot more options in the game now than in the past." One of those options was the international tie-breaker rule, which was first used in the National Sports Festival in Syracuse New York, in 1981 and helped to speed up the game if the score was tied after seven innings.

In 1973, the IJRCS consolidated the twelve-inch slow-pitch and fast-pitch rules. "This is a major step forward and will bring uniformity in umpiring, protest handling and interpretations," said George Cron, chairman of the IJRCS. Tom Mason, IJRCS rules interpreter, said, "There is no doubt that the combining of the slow- and fast-pitch rules will be of great help to the umpires as well and make interpretations much easier. Also, the changes and maintaining the rules will be made much easier in the future. It will also cut down printing costs considerably."

By 1980, the ASA had taken over as the rules-governing body of softball in the United States, and today the committee meets annually to discuss and pass the rules proposals submitted by members of the ASA National Council. In recent years, they have discussed fewer rule proposals at each meeting, but it is unclear if that trend will continue. Kevin Ryan, ASA supervisor of umpires, said, "I am not sure that the number of rules will be less or more. Each year the members of the Council look at the problem areas and submit rule changes to try and help the game of softball.

"Because our rules cover several games (fastpitch, slow-pitch, sixteen-inch slow-pitch and modified pitch), the number of rules will and should vary each year. As the athletes get better, the suggestions that rule changes be accepted to adapt to the athletes will continue. Also, as the game expands the rules seem to be adapted so more folks can play. I believe this will continue over the years."

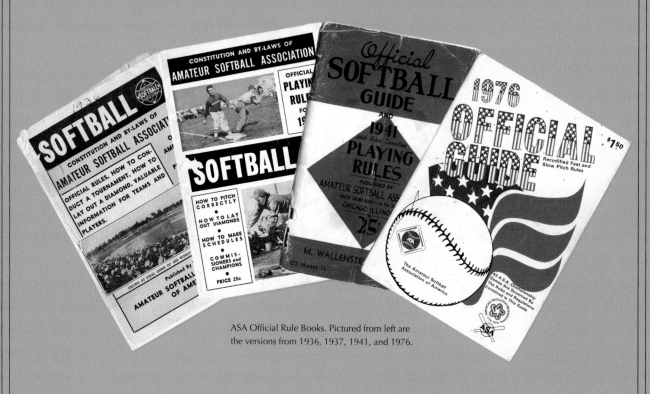

ASA Official Rule Books. Pictured from left are the versions from 1936, 1937, 1941, and 1976.

Fischer and Pauley's organization held their next meeting in 1934, at which time they voted Clarence Brewer of Detroit, Michigan, to be chairman, and they decided to incorporate the body into a "not for profit" organization. The meeting in Chicago was attended by nearly 200 representatives of organizations interested in softball. To help get the 1934 tournament started, Pauley and Fischer obtained $7,000 from William Randolph Hearst to help defray the cost of hotel rooms and to provide a little entertainment for the 1,001 team members who played in the Chicago tournament. Teams were still required to pick up their own travel-related costs. In addition to the financial support he provided, Hearst promoted the event through his newspaper, and contributed a total of $50,000 through 1938. The Chicago Park District also helped out, setting up the diamonds at no expense.

Thirty-two teams representing twenty-five states competed in the tournament. All of the games were played during the day. In the end, the Ke-Nash-A Motormakers of Kenosha, Wisconsin, defeated the Crimson Coaches of Toledo, Ohio, in the men's finale, 2–0; and the Hart Motor Girls of Chicago defeated Gem City of Dayton, Ohio in the women's championship, 5–1. The Wisconsin team received the William Randolph Hearst Trophy, which was thirty-seven inches in height, with ball and figures of solid gold and ebony, valued at $1,000.

The 1934 tournament brought in more than 200,000 people in three days. Just as with the previous tournament, admission was free. Among those attending the championship were the czar of baseball, Judge Kenesaw Mountain Landis, and his wife. Landis made his mark as baseball's first commissioner by banning for life eight players who earlier had been acquitted in the "Black Sox" scandal of 1919. With his leadership, Landis restored the reputation

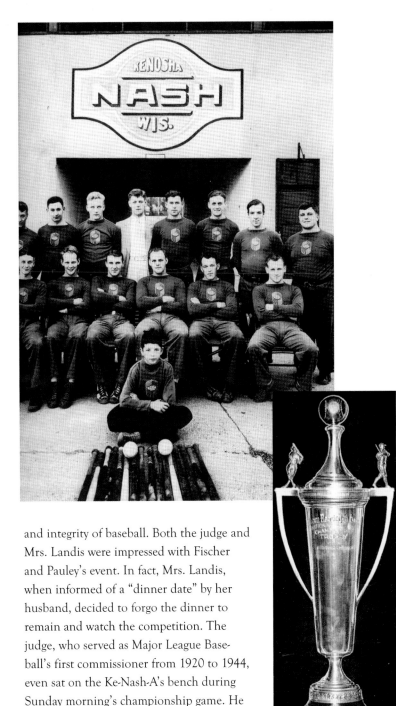

and integrity of baseball. Both the judge and Mrs. Landis were impressed with Fischer and Pauley's event. In fact, Mrs. Landis, when informed of a "dinner date" by her husband, decided to forgo the dinner to remain and watch the competition. The judge, who served as Major League Baseball's first commissioner from 1920 to 1944, even sat on the Ke-Nash-A's bench during Sunday morning's championship game. He told the *Chicago American* that he "didn't believe [softball] would hurt baseball. On the contrary, he explained, "Any game that can interest fans is bound to help the enthusiasm for any sport."

At one point in the event, Landis asked Rip Collins, a member of the Gas House Gang (a nickname for the St. Louis

Top: the Ke-Nash-A Motormakers, 1934 ASA National Champions.
Bottom: the William Randolph Hearst trophy.

The Bendix Brakes men's team of South Bend, IN fully understood the value of advertising, and used the names of different products on their jerseys, rather than numbers.

Cardinals), "Ripper, do you think you could hit that big ball?"

"Pardon the expression, Judge," said Collins, "but hell, I can't even see it."

ASA members saw the tournament, which was attended by twenty-two ASA commissioners, as an opportunity to offer some recommendations on how to improve the game. These recommendations were as follows: increasing the men's pitching distance from 37 feet 8 ½ inches to forty feet, as a way of getting more offense into the game; enlarging the scope of the ASA; and again holding the tournament in Chicago. "The years of persistent effort, constant promotion and unchanging faith of the believers in softball proved to have not been in vain, for in 1934 softball came into its own," proclaimed the *Playground Association Softball Guide* in 1935. "All over America hundreds of leagues and thousands of players enthusiastically accepted this major team game."

The Guide continued: "The promotional activities of the Amateur Softball Association of America played an important part in stimulating the interest that had been developing for many years. The battle for recognition of this splendid sport is over.

Softball has won a place among America's foremost sports."

The 1934 championship was a major turning point for the ASA. As Fischer wrote, "The tournament also served to put firmly on the map the Amateur Softball Association of America, which in one year has stepped forward to be recognized as the governing body of the sport, with affiliated bodies in 35 states, with others certain to line up before the next year." Later he added, "It was through the efforts of Hearst newspapers and others that state championship tournaments were held throughout the country to determine qualifiers for the national meet." It was official—the 1933 tournament got the group off the ground, and the 1934 tournament established the ASA as an organization.

1936 will be remembered as the year that Rochester, New York's Harold "Shifty" Gears, who in 1957 would become the first inductee into the ASA National Softball Hall of Fame, led Kodak Park through the rain to the men's title, thereby making his the first eastern team to win the event. Despite ending up $7,547.57 in the red after that championship, the ASA made progress and established associations in forty-one of the forty-eight states, plus ten metro associations. Nationwide, the ASA estimated that in the United States 92,545 teams played 1,850,000 games in front of 185,090,000 people. On the field, the ASA had by now recognized the twelve-inch, smooth-seam ball as their official ball, abandoned the forty-five-foot diamond for the sixty-foot diamond, and increased the pitching distance to forty feet, as members had suggested in 1934.

During the 1936 tournament, the ASA elected sectional vice-presidents for the first time. Named were Walter Hakanson of Denver, Colorado (Western); Harold B. Dow of Westport, Connecticut (Eastern); Early Maxwell of Memphis, Tennessee (Southern); and Seth Whitmore of Lansing, Michigan (Central). In an effort to pull itself out of the red, the ASA sought financial assistance from the *Chicago American*. The newspaper agreed, under the condition that the sum

be deducted from the 1937 championship proceeds prior to any profit being realized.

The 1937 men's championship was highlighted by the fastest men's game played in ASA National Championship play. Norbert "Cyclone" Warken (deceased), pitcher for Curlee Clothing Company of Covington, Kentucky, took only twenty-seven minutes to defeat Denver, Colorado, 3–0, striking out fourteen and allowing one hit while facing twenty-two batters. Curlee finished fifth in the championship, with Warken striking out sixty-six batters in four games and pitching two no-hitters (including the tournament's only perfect game) in the same day.

Continued on page 16

Clockwise from top right: the 1936 ASA National Champion team, Kodak Park of Rochester, NY; Harold "Shifty" Gears, Kodak Park's pitcher; Hank Kremble, Kodak Park's second baseman.

Balls and Strikes

Realizing communication would be a key to the success of the newly founded ASA, Leo Fischer said, "We need a bulletin to send out each month to the newly-formed Amateur Softball Association's commissioners." The idea for that bulletin turned into *Balls and Strikes*. First produced in mimeograph form, using a stencil, the one-page sheet was issued from "time to time in the interests of the association and the game."

The early issues contained information about what was happening in the local associations, with comments by the local association commissioners on how softball was progressing in their association.

In 1937, a special issue highlighting the world championships was produced. By January of 1939, the publication *Softball* was started in Lansing, Michigan,

Balls and Strikes was originally an internal communications tool for the ASA. It eventually became the organization's official publication.

by the Michigan ASA. Seth Whitmore of Lansing was the original editor and sponsor of the newspaper, which the ASA sanctioned as their official publication. The publication included news of the Amateur Softball Association in a regular column with the title "Soft Balls and Strikes," which later was shortened to "Balls and Strikes." The newsletter, which sold for 10 cents, had an average circulation of 6,100 readers.

The name *Softball* eventually became *Softball News*, which continued to devote a full page to the ASA until June of 1942, when the ASA Board of Directors chose to shut it down. Still needing to communicate with its members, the ASA switched back to using a mimeograph to produce its publication. By April 1947 the ASA saw fit to give the publication another at-bat, this time in a newspaper format, with a front-page headline declaring "*Balls and Strikes* celebrates birthday by becoming a newspaper." For a while at least, members could look forward to their ASA news coming in a four-page, seven-column, broadsheet publication.

Increasing operating costs forced the ASA to again revert back to the mimeograph following the August 1948 issue. In that issue Pauley wrote an editorial about the swan song of both *Balls And Strikes* and himself as editor "because of the increase in the price of newsprint (paper) and labor charges." *Balls And Strikes* remained in mimeograph form for a few months (November–December 1948), however, until it was changed to a four-column, and then a five-column tabloid. *Balls and Strikes* remained a tabloid from May–June 1949 until switching to a coated-stock magazine in May–June 1980.

In addition to publishing *Balls and Strikes*, from time-to-time, beginning with the December 1969 issue, the ASA produced a magazine entitled *ASA Softball*. In 1982, the ASA switched *Balls and Strikes*

Clockwise from top left:
Covers of *Balls and Strikes* from 1937, 1982, 2000, and 2008.

back to a four-column tabloid, and kept the publication in that form until 1996, when they attempted to again publish the bulletin as a magazine.

It was the beginning of the end, however, for the ASA's official publication, with rising costs and decreasing advertising revenues contributing to its downfall. By 1999, the ASA reduced the publication of *Balls and Strikes* from five issues per year to two—a season preview in February and a national championship/season recap issue in the fall. On March 1, 1999, the ASA launched the first online issue of *Balls and Strikes* on its Web site, and it is currently published on a limited basis.

The ASA also publishes an official in-house newsletter, *The Inside Pitch*, first printed in 1996. This publication is sent electronically at least eleven times per year, to members of the ASA National Council and others involved with the ASA. Due to its limited distribution, its advertising is made up primarily of house ads. It contains no paid advertising.

Walter Hakanson

Walter Hakanson, one of the ASA's pioneers, had an exceptional career in sports. Prior to serving as ASA president in 1948, he held a joint position as both commissioner and secretary-treasurer for the Colorado ASA. He was instrumental in rule-writing and in formulating the constitution and bylaws of the ASA, and he officially founded the Colorado ASA in 1931, although he had run state tournaments organized by the YMCA since 1926. Furthermore, Hakanson was an accomplished athlete (three times all-city in football and four times all-city in basketball), a skilled basketball (2,284 games) and football (445 games) official for twenty-five years, and an outstanding administrator during his forty-five-year career with the Denver YMCA. He was involved in numerous other sports including gymnastics, basketball, football, swimming, volleyball, handball, and baseball. And for eight years, he had a calisthenics exercise program broadcast over radio station KLZ, despite the fact that he smoked a pack of cigarettes a day.

It was ultimately in softball that Hakanson achieved national recognition. In fact, Hakanson gave the sport its name at a 1926 Colorado Softball Committee meeting in Greeley, Colorado. Hakanson saw that in each state throughout the country the sport had a different name and was played by slightly different rules. He knew that in order for the sport to flourish, it badly needed a single recognizable name. So that year Commissioner Hakanson proposed that the committee agree to use the name "softball." The committee adopted the name from among many others, such as "mush ball," "kitten ball," "diamond ball," and "playground ball." It wasn't until 1932, when Hakanson attended a Chicago committee meeting intended to codify and unify the rules of this popular game, that the name softball gained national acceptance.

Hakanson, who retired from the YMCA on December 1, 1962, said in a newspaper article that "Softball enjoyed its greatest season in history in 1946 and the Amateur Softball Association anticipated even greater things [in 1947]." He also said that "Recreation and public officials are working diligently to keep up with the demand for diamonds. Two hundred and thirty-nine cities constructed seven hundred and seventy-one diamonds last season [1946], yet they could not appease the cry, 'Give us more places to play'."

The championships were proving to be quite popular for those who played and attended them, but they still weren't money-makers. After the 1937 tournament, the ASA once again sought financial assistance from the *Chicago American*, which paid the $1,062.87 deficit realized from the 1937 World Championships.

By 1938, the ASA established its Board of Governors (later known as the Executive Board or Board of Directors), and assigned President Fischer duties as chairman of that board during a meeting on September 9, 1939, at the Morrison Hotel. After serving as president since its inception, Fischer later retired that same year, with the ASA showing a deficit of only $621.36, money owed Pauley, who had been elected secretary-treasurer for a seventh consecutive term. In announcing his retirement, Fischer felt the ASA was being used for the promotion of a commercial product, which he was against.

In a letter to President Landis, dated April 13, 1941, Fischer wrote: "I would like to go on record at the spring meeting against the proposed tie-up with Pepsi-Cola or any organization sponsoring a commercial product for our world's championship tournament. Regardless of the need for financial aid, it would be a very serious back step for the organization.

"Although the *Herald-American* spent close to $30,000 in staging the first six world's championship meets, I felt it was a big advance when you induced us to move

the tournament to Detroit with the promise of civic backing—even though this newspaper never asked anything from the ASA except goodwill. It was also a great step forward when we eliminated the ASA official ball, despite the fact that it necessitated the current subsidization by sporting goods manufacturers.

"The world's championship meet is the top event of our entire annual program. It is as inconceivable as it would be to have Coca-Cola sponsor the baseball World Series or Royal Crown the Olympic Games. I like to drink Pepsi-Cola and that company is to be commended for its interest in softball and other amateur sports, but you can be certain that underwriting the world's championship is not being done from a purely altruistic standpoint. Their advertising men are put in the same class with other promotion, such as sky-writing, magazine ads, etc., used to aid the sale of Pepsi-Cola.

"I, for one, feel that the highest honor in amateur softball should not be made on the basis of a sale promotion for a soft drink—not any commercial product, regardless of its merits."

Left: opening ceremonies with parade of teams at 1938 ASA National Championship in Chicago.
Below: the 1938 ASA Commissioners Council meeting at the Morrison Hotel in Chicago.

CHAPTER II

1940s

OVERCOMING THE
DEPRESSION

While the Depression defined the 1930s, World War II (1939–1945) defined the 1940s. And although the U.S. finally overcame the Depression, its effects hung on into the early 1940s, when the U.S. entered the war and the government began drafting young men and spending more on its military. The war efforts created a new market of civilian jobs in the defense and war industries, helping to pull the U.S. out of the Depression.

Even with the war, and with the U.S. emerging as a world superpower, the ASA surged forward following Fischer's retirement, thanks to the leadership of Wilbur E. "Judge" Landis and Raymond Johnson of Nashville, Tennessee. Less than a decade old, the ASA named M.J. Pauley secretary-treasurer for a seventh consecutive term and elected Landis, of Detroit, Michigan, president in 1940.

Landis had played a major role in the development of softball for the Briggs Beautyware Company, which won ASA national fast-pitch titles in 1937, '48, '52 and '53. He introduced softball to Briggs as a morale

booster, and before long other industrial companies had their own softball programs. When Landis joined the Industrial Relations Division of Detroit's Briggs Manufacturing Company in 1928, their company-sponsored athletics program consisted of one baseball team. By the mid '40s, the program had expanded to more than 400 bowling teams, 100 softball teams, and numerous other teams in golf, tennis, basketball, and a myriad of other sports. In 1934, Landis organized the Industrial Association of Detroit. Eventually more than thirty-seven industrial firms, representing 210,000 Motor City workers, were

Facing page: members of the Deep Rock Oilers of Tulsa, OK, arrive in Chicago prior to winning the 1942 ASA National Championship.
Left: Wilbur E. Landis of Detroit (standing), president of the ASA, presenting the 1941 World's Softball Championship official Ford Mercury car to ASA Executive Secretary M.J. Pauley (in car). The car was painted red (bottom), white (stripe), and blue (top).

19

members of the association, which promoted inter-company competition in softball, golf, boxing, basketball, hockey, tennis, and other team sports. In 1940, Landis was first elected ASA president, and he was re-elected in '41 and '42. He declined the nomination in '43 but remained as Detroit commissioner.

While many appreciated what Landis did during his term of office, Raymond Johnson proved to be the right man at the right time for the ASA. If not for Johnson, the ASA could have just as easily folded. Raymond Johnson could be gruff but polite. And his handshake, backbone, and management style were all the same—firm. He was known as "crusty on the outside but soft on the inside" by his press box buddies. And he liked nothing better than to light up a half-chewed, Dutch Master cigar. "If there was an angel for the ASA, it was Raymond Johnson," Buck Johnson, former sports editor of the *Chattanooga Times* and a long-time friend of Johnson, said.

Johnson took office as ASA president following the 1942 World's Championship, with "plenty of zip, vim and vigor," as Pauley wrote in the Annual Report of the Executive

Secretary. Johnson started his relationship with the ASA in 1937 and marked his fiftieth year in the sport during the centennial year of softball in 1987.

Acting as sports editor of the *Tennessean*, Raymond Johnson told the commissioners on September 19, 1942, inside the Fort Shelby Hotel in Detroit that he "would do his best to uphold the dignity of his office and asked for the cooperation of each and every commissioner." Johnson, who would serve the longest term as president in the history of the association (September 19, 1942, to January 18, 1948), then asked for a "rising vote of thanks to Landis for the time and effort he spent during the years (1940–42) he was in the president's chair."

He added "No one was more surprised than I was on September 18, 1942, when I was told that I would become the ASA president the next morning. I was supposed to cover the Georgia-Kentucky football game in Louisville on September 19 and the Southern League playoffs starting the next afternoon," Johnson said. "I switched from the trains to planes to get from Detroit to Louisville to Little Rock. But that's getting ahead of the story.

"I was scared when told by a committee headed by James Rooney that I was to be the president. I was pleased, too. Then late that night as Johnny Deaver, Herb Pailet, Bob Shelton and Gene Martin talked, I was warned that I was sticking my neck out.

"My fears increased the next morning. Almost as if it was a pre-arranged signal, the Detroit air-raid sirens went off as Wilbur Landis handed me the gavel in the roof garden of Detroit's Fort Shelby Hotel. It was very foggy outside.

"The fog had the planes grounded and I had to wire my office that it was impossible for me to cover the football game in Louisville, but that I would be in Little Rock the next day. I took a train to Cincinnati, another to St. Louis. I was supposed to get

DID YOU KNOW?
. . . .

Battle of the Sexes

Throughout history, sports have had the "Battle of the Sexes," matching men against women. The ASA proved it was not immune from this battle when, on March 12, 1940, four men's players matched wits against five women's players on NBC radio's Molle Shaving Cream's "Battle of the Sexes" program. The participants, hand-picked by then ASA vice president Gene Martin, all came from New Jersey's 1939 championship teams. The girls were from the Linden-Arians, of Linden, New Jersey, while the men came from the Elgins. The players were asked questions strictly related to softball.

one from St. Louis to Little Rock, but since we arrived late, the Arkansas-bound train was gone. I finally got a plane to Memphis, then a bus to Little Rock. A PFC bounced me off the plane from Memphis to Little Rock.

"I went from the bus station to the baseball park. It was the last of the ninth inning, two out, when I walked in with my typewriter in one hand and my handbag in the other. Fortunately, the score was 0–0. Nashville won 1–0 in ten innings, Paul Erickson beating Ed Lopat. I got my story."

In reminiscing about his years as president, Raymond Johnson recalled that one commissioner felt he had made a mistake in accepting the presidency because, as was the commissioner's opinion, the ASA would die during the war. "And if it did, I would be the goat," said Johnson in the *1948 ASA Official Guide.* Johnson continued, stating, "The ASA, however, not only survived but came out of the war the largest amateur athletic organization in the world in the number of registered participants. Softball grew in this country and the seeds the GIs sowed on the battlefields of the world have enabled the game to grow in popularity that it is now played around the world."

Approximately 67,000 teams participated in elimination tournaments held in encampments and bases throughout the United States in 1942. In 1943, despite the armed forces' demand for men and material during World War II, the ASA grew, allowing only regional championships. Additionally, the tremendous drain on manpower forced many civilian teams to suspend play for the duration, as the armed forces called entire squads into battle. Defense plants formed softball teams on a large scale, thus helping to offset the loss of civilian teams. In the end, the gigantic service program was a boon to softball.

Wrote Johnson in the *1944 Guide,* "The young men in the service have carried softball

The manager and captain of the Tip Top Tailors of Toronto, Canada, presenting the Friendship and Goodwill Award to ASA President Wilbur E. Landis (left) and MI Governor Murray D. Van Wagoner at the Pageant of American Youth (opening night of 1941 World's Championship).

to practically every corner of the world and as a result if this spreading of the softball gossip, the game is certain to be bigger and greater when peace comes to the world again. We have had letters from friends in the service telling of softball games in North Africa that attracted 6,000 spectators; of games in the Aleutians that drew practically every available man not on duty; of games in New Guinea, Guadalcanal, Sicily, Italy, England, China, Australia, Iceland and practically every Allied country. Maj. Gen. Clair L. Chennault took time out from his army duties in China to pitch a softball game for his bomber base last May. His team won, 17–5."

By 1945, according to that year's *ASA Guide,* "There was a decrease of approximately 18,000 service teams in the United States in 1944, but nearly 49,000 participated

Continued on page 24

Softball in the Armed Forces

Softball participation in the armed forces dates back to 1934 to the Naval Air Station team, which had, according to Morris Bealle, "a dazzling spinball pitcher named Hank Collins." While the servicemen helped to popularize softball overseas during World War II, in time, nearly every company, wing, flight, office, or squad had a softball team. Because of the war, there was a drain on manpower, causing the dismantling of thousands of civilian teams. The shortage of civilian teams, however, was made up for by hundreds of defense plant clubs and 67,000 service teams.

With fast-pitch the game of choice, service teams eagerly anticipated participating in the ASA Men's Major Fast-Pitch National Championship. The renowned Hammer Field Raiders, of Fresno, California, the only service team to win an ASA National Championship, won back-to-back titles in 1943 and 1944, with Hall of Fame pitchers Al Linde and Kermit Lynch leading the way.

One of the best finishes for the Armed Forces men's team came in 1969 when they finished third (3–2) in the Men's Major Fast-Pitch National Championship, with Stratford, Connecticut, and Mt. View, California, finishing ahead of them. Two members of the armed forces, Don Dungee and Charles Acklin, were named first-team All-America, with Stan Baker and George Giles named to the second-team.

Two more of the best showings for armed forces teams came in

1966 when the Air Force finished eighth and the Navy seventh. In 1968, the armed forces finished thirteenth in the Men's Major Fast-Pitch National Championship. In 1971, the armed forces finished seventh in the Men's Major Fast-Pitch National Championship, followed by a sixth-place finish in 1972 and a twelfth-place finish in 1973. In 1975, the U.S.M.C. armed forces finished fourteenth. In 1976, the armed forces had one team, which finished ninth in the Men's Major Fast-Pitch National Championship.

Linde and Lynch weren't the only Hall of Fame pitchers who starred in the armed forces. Others included David Scott (Air Force), Bill Massey (Air

ASA officials (from left to right) John Deaver, president; George Dickstein, umpire-in-chief, and B.E. (Gene) Martin, executive secretary-treasurer, are greeted by Maj. J. Smith (right), chief of the USAFE Special Services Division, at Rhein/Main Air Base, Germany. The three ASA officials conducted a softball training school, April 8–12, 1957 at Landsberg, Air Base. (USAF Photo)

Force), Roy "Burly" Burlison (Navy), Johnny Spring (Army), Harvey Sterkel (Navy) and Joe Lynch (Navy).

Scott went 1–1 in his first ASA national pitching for Lackland AFB in San Antonio before deciding to settle in Decatur, Illinois, and lead that community to fast-pitch prominence. Two of the pitchers in the Navy with Burlison were Ted Brown and Jim Cheeseman, who went 1–2 in the 1965 ASA Men's Major Fast-Pitch National.

In 1952, the Air Force was the first of the armed forces to affiliate with the ASA and determined its entry through world-wide tournaments and participated in ASA tournaments in 1952, l953, l954, 1955, 1956, 1957, 1959, 1960, and 1966.

In 1953, the Navy went 0–2 in the national in Miami, with Sterkel taking the losses, allowing eight runs on eight hits in 11 1/3 innings. The Air Force was represented by Elmendorf AFB, which split four games.

In 1954, the Navy joined the ASA but didn't send a team, while the Army, which had been conducting its worldwide tournament too late in the year to determine a team for the ASA, first participated in 1957 and finished tied for eighth.

Although men primarily played in the ASA Men's Major Fast-Pitch National Championship, the first time the Navy women played in the Women's Major National Championships was in 1954 in Orange, California. The Navy's women's team was the San Diego Naval Airbase Skyraiders, who were winless in two games. Despite their poor record, they did have the winner of Miss Softball, second baseman Margaret Cozad, who received a diamond ring and an orchid from TV star Spade Cooley.

Gradually, fast-pitch declined because of a lack of pitchers, and the armed forces turned to slow-pitch. The armed forces men's slow-pitch team finished runner-up in the ASA Men's Major Slow-Pitch National Championship in Sanford, Florida, in 2005, and competed in the Class A Slow-Pitch National Championship in 2007. Softball players-turned-servicemen more than did their share to help promote and develop softball abroad. Without them, softball would have never gained international popularity to become a worldwide sport played by millions.

When fast-pitch was the game of choice in the Armed Services, the Strategic Air Command of Offutt, AFB, Nebraska could be counted on to have an excellent team.

in the ASA program. The ASA assisted more than 1,200 schools with approximately 30,000 boys' and girls' teams in sponsoring softball during the year. The civilian teams numbered approximately 215,000, with the majority of them being in war plants."

Following the Germans' surrender on May 7, 1945, the engineer units, which normally built combat bridges and airfields, transformed the battlefields of Europe into ball fields, according to Gary Bedingfield in the introduction of Baseball in World War II Europe. Wrote Bedingfield, "Never before had there been an athletic program of such magnitude. The amount of equipment required was colossal, and shortly after VE Day, the War Department in Washington, D.C., made available 85,964 ball gloves, 72,850 baseballs and 131,130 bats. By mid-summer 200,000 troops were playing in competitive leagues, military duties were scheduled around games and combat units temporarily put aside the emotional and physical scars of recent battles in their pursuit to be the best team in their region."

Servicemen, especially the POWs, did what they had to do to take their minds off the rigors of the war. In the long run, both baseball and softball benefited, especially where softball and baseball fields were built after the servicemen returned home when the war ended. Roger Long, resident of New Market, Iowa, and POW in World War II for twenty-seven months, told writer Jan Castle Renander, "We played a lot of cards. I read the Bible from front page to back page. We made our own softball, out of an unraveled sock. You can do anything you set your mind to."

Some of the servicemen even played in German prison camps. In the *1945 ASA Guide*, Johnson wrote, "Frank Maxwell, who worked with 'Believe-It-Or-Not' Bob Ripley before Pearl Harbor, told of a group of Americans in the same camp with him making a ball and bat by hand in order that they might

get to play. 'We found softball was the best thing possible in order to get our minds off our troubles while prisoners,' Maxwell said."

As a testament to softball's steadfastness during the war, ASA President Fred Crosby wrote (in February 1960), "Softball became of age and emerged on the horizon of sports as an organization with purposeful aims and objectives. These were war years, grim and frightening, with mass movements of people, the youth engulfed by the armed forces, the civilians absorbed by industry. The nation looked for an interesting sport for diversion, relaxation, inexpensive and easy to play.

"Softball met these qualifications and became one of the most popular sports with our armed forces on bases and camps throughout the world. Industry realized the value for the release of tensions and clean, healthy recreation. Industrial and city-wide recreational leagues for men, women, boys and girls sprang up all over the nation. The nation needed softball and softball needed the nation."

Johnson, however, credited the ASA's wartime success to the commissioners, "who did a wonderful job," and to Coca-Cola. In reference to the commissioners, he wrote, "The presidency of softball has meant much to me and I shall never forget those who were responsible for bestowing the honor upon me. I leave the chair with many fond memories of contacts and of associations with men in many walks of life throughout the United States, Canada, Mexico and Puerto Rico."

In reference to Coca-Cola, Johnson would later write, "The Coca-Cola people were wonderful to us from the first time I mentioned the possibility of Coca-Cola sponsoring softball to the late Bill Kaliska in December, 1942."

According to Johnson, Coca-Cola, via their promotions director, William Kaliska, donated in excess of $10,000 to buy trophies and help with office postage in 1943, and the company donated $5,000 more for office operations. In rounding out the donations the ASA received that year, the Morrison Hotel donated office space, and Johnson's newspaper paid his expenses. Kaliska liked the promotion and after repeating it in 1944, he upped the donation to $15,000 in 1946.

The ASA's ties with soft-drink companies began in 1941, when Pepsi-Cola initially sponsored the World's Softball Championships. The agreement between the ASA and Pepsi-Cola was announced at the spring meeting of the ASA on April 19, 1941, at the Leland Hotel in Chicago. In making the announcement, Secretary Pauley said that the "Pepsi-Cola Company was to give each state or metro association, in good standing, a 30-inch trophy with a $50.00 retail value, to their men's champion. The same would also be given to each state or metro girl's champ whose entry fee into the world's championship had been paid by the national treasury. The world champion trophies, team and individual, are also to be given by the Pepsi-Cola Company."

In 1941, the ASA had more than 300,000 players competing and more than one-hundred million fans witnessed games, according to president Wilbur Landis, writing in the *1942 Guide.*

A letter from the president of Pepsi-Cola, Walter S. Mack, also was read to the group. In it, Mack said it was "indeed a pleasure for the Pepsi-Cola Company to be associated with the ASA as sponsor of the 1941 World Amateur Softball Championships. We are fully aware of the esteemed reputation your association now enjoys and we are confident that this tournament will uphold the standards of clean sportsmanship and hard competition that had prevailed in the past." A year later, however, Pepsi-Cola didn't renew its option to sponsor the awards for the 1942 championships because of a lack of cooperation by the state and metro commissioners,

according to Pauley in a memo to the commissioners on February 16, 1942.

That year, Pauley also used ASA funds to pay off more than $7,000 in debts it had incurred, some of it due since 1938, leaving nothing in the ASA bank account. Except for the back salary ($8,860) it owed Pauley as executive secretary from 1940 through 1942, the association wasn't "indebted to any individual or firm for one cent."

A major change for tournament formatting also came in 1942. Because wartime travel restrictions made it necessary for the ASA to limit the number of teams

Left: the Higgins Midgets of Tulsa, OK, watch from the dugout during the 1941 ASA Championship in Detroit, MI. Nina Korgan (on the left end of bench) pitched her team to the national title.
Below: department store display shows the trophy for the 1941 ASA National Championships.

The 1942 championship was held September 10–14 at the University of Detroit Stadium with the double-elimination format used for the first time. The Deep Rock Oilers of Tulsa, OK, and the Nina Korgan-led Jax Maids were the respective men's and women's champions.

participating in a single tournament, they divided the United States into fifteen regions and held regional tournaments to keep travel at a minimum. Through reducing the number of teams in the national tournament, held that year in Detroit, the ASA was able to hold a double-knockout or double-elimination national championship instead of a single-elimination event, as had been the norm since the organization began.

The double-elimination format was such a big hit with the teams that the ASA decided to use it from that year forward. Some teams, especially northwestern teams who didn't participate in the previous single-elimination tournaments because travel expenses couldn't be justified by being sent home after just one loss, had new reason to participate. In fact, one team from the northwest (Dunn Lumber of Seattle) didn't participate in the championship until 1940. The double-elimination format has remained popular to this day, although the number of local associations has decreased through the years.

Throughout these early years, the war was taking its toll on the sport of softball and the ASA. In the *1946 ASA Guide*, Johnson recalled those first years as president and the gloom and doom some had predicted for softball: "Many pictured the future of softball as dark and dismal in September 1942 when we took office. The war clouds were the darkest

then and it was predicted that all sports would have to shut down until the hostilities had ceased.

"Out of the global conflict came softball with a following no other sport has enjoyed. Men and women in all branches of the armed forces played the game in practically every country in the world. It gave them pleasant memories and enabled them to forget the serious side of war momentarily."

On the war front, softball's future was bright because the army-navy special department sent five times as much softball equipment abroad to our troops than all athletic ware, according to *The Spokesman-Review*, August 19, 1945.

Half the baseball players had enlisted by 1943, leaving teams with older veterans. Additionally, by 1943 the war had increased and caused the disbanding of thousands of men's civilian teams. This shortage, however, was made up with numerous defense plant teams and 67,000 service teams. Women's teams during this time remained intact, and some traveled to military bases to play exhibition games against the troops.

1943 was a bad year financially for the ASA, as it had budgeting problems and was $12,132.47 in the red when the Spring Commissioners' Meeting convened at the Carter Hotel in Cleveland, Ohio, from April

Continued on page 28

Doubting the Validity of the ASA

In the ASA's infancy, there were some who doubted it would last even a few years, let alone the seventy-five years needed to celebrate a diamond jubilee. But, as attested to by Seth Whitmore in the January 1940 issue of *Softball,* "The effort of a few to discredit the ASA failed. At the National AAU convention the executive board of that body voted unanimously to continue the alliance with the ASA and lauded our association for its record."

The ASA's foothold as a governing body was recognized by other sporting organizations, including the American Softball Association, a professional league run by George Sisler. "There is every indication that friction will be at a very minimum in 1940 and organized softball will march forward to greater peaks than any previously reached," wrote Whitmore in his column, "Softball Servings."

Speaking at the annual banquet of the Michigan Softball Association on March 9, 1940, L.H. Weir, director of park recreation planning for the National Recreation Association and former circuit judge in

Cincinnati, described softball as a "major factor tending toward continuance of American democracy."

Weir also said "Softball parks are cheaper to build and maintain and will build stronger character than penal institutions," and that the next major development in softball would be in the "wide open spaces" or rural areas. "The federal electrification program has brought electric power into all parts of the nation, and today we find lighted softball playing fields springing up in farming centers," he said.

He pointed out how the development of recreation centers in Cincinnati ended delinquency and stopped a wave of crime among boys in numerous neighborhoods.

Weir predicted that, because of the demand for increased recreational facilities, one day the thirty-hour work week would become a reality. Weir's prediction, as history has shown, never materialized, but softball certainly filled the void for leisure-time activities, and the Amateur Softball Association led the way.

The ASA National Council meeting is popular with commissioners and members of their staff who plan softball for the coming year. At its peak, the ASA had 110 local associations. In 2008, the ASA numbers 83 local associations throughout the United States.

Below left: 2008 Hall of Fame inductee Kermit Lynch was not only an outstanding pitcher but he was lethal with the bat, driving in the game's only run in the 1943 championship game for the Hammer Field Raiders.

Below right: the 1944 ASA National Championship team: Hammer Field Raiders of Fresno, CA. ASA Hall-of-Famers Al Linde and Kermit Lynch (front row, second and fourth from left, respectively) also led the Raiders to the national title in 1943. Linde hurled 1944 championship game with Lynch doing the honors in 1943.

22–23, 1944. In fact, the committee, chaired by James Rhodes of Columbus, Ohio, met with the sole intent of pulling the association out of the red. Rhodes recommended that each team be assessed $2 in addition to their regular entry fee or membership fee charged by the state or metro associations. The commissioners approved the plan and, starting with the season's district-level tournaments, assessed the teams with the one-time fee. At the meeting, Secretary Pauley pointed out that by selling ten sustaining ASA memberships at $25 per year, the commissioners could raise another $4,000 for the ASA.

Many of the service teams played in civilian leagues and tournaments near their bases. One such team was the Hammer Field Raiders, which won game after game while playing in the San Joaquin Valley and San Francisco Bay Region. The team had two outstanding pitchers, Private Al Linde, who later was elected into the ASA National Softball Hall of Fame, and Sergeant Kermit Lynch, now an Oklahoma City resident and 2008 inductee into the ASA Hall of Fame. These two men helped the team win the Pacific Coast Regional before moving on to the national championship.

For a while, however, it appeared that the Raiders wouldn't get to the national championship. Getting permission from officials in Washington was almost impossible. When they finally got permission, the players had another problem, as they couldn't find sponsorship for their transportation. But at a special meeting, the Hammer Field Officers' Club donated $2,500 to pay for the travel to the tournament. If the Officers' Club hadn't come through, there was a "Minute Man" Committee of local patriotic Fresnans ready to step forward to defray the travel costs. Handling the adversity paid off on September 21 when, in front of 5,000 fans in Detroit Stadium with Lynch as pitcher, the Raiders (5–1) prevailed over Detroit's Briggs Bombers.

The Raiders repeated in 1944, with Linde nipping a determined Fort Wayne, Indiana, Zollner Piston team, 1–0, in Cleveland, Ohio, at Elks Stadium. Linde called beating the Pistons in the semis and finals

"The greatest thrill of his career."

The Lakewood Elks Club underwrote the tournament and provided the stadium a lit field, a cover for the grandstand and bleachers, an electric scoreboard, and a public address system. Previously, Jack O'Malia, chairman of the Elks Club Sports Committee, conceived of introducing lights to the stadium while visiting Havana, Cuba, which he did in 1932. In 1934, the neighborhood residents sued the Elks Club, claiming night softball was a nuisance. The judge disagreed and threw the case out, ruling that night softball was good entertainment—provided there was a reasonable curfew. The stadium, where O'Malia had started holding softball games in 1925, hosted five ASA National Championships (1944–1948). 1948 was O'Malia's last year at Elks Field, although the stadium existed until 1958, when it was shut down and replaced by a chain store in 1959. In 1943, a year before the first nationals were held at Elks Stadium, the ASA national office had an operating loss of $1,470.30, with expenses of $15,531.28 and income of $14,060.98. The association owed Pauley an additional $10,330.85 in back salary for 1940 ($366.35), 1941 ($4,158.00), 1942 ($4,336.20), and 1943 ($1,470.30). And the 1943 World Championships reflected a net loss of $4,080.97

The ASA began to see a financial turnaround in 1944, however, when the World's Tournament realized a profit of $4,366.20, with the East Central Regional profiting $2,307.34. The Lakewood Athletic Commission assigned half of this amount ($1,153.67) to pay for bats, balls, and umpires' fees, then submitted the remainder to the ASA national treasury.

That 1944 tournament was the first of five held at Elks Stadium. In 1946, the Metro Cleveland ASA asked the Lakewood Elks Club to make improvements to the field. The Lakewood Elks agreed, provided Cleveland would host the tournament for five years. In turn, Cleveland agreed, and the Elks spent $30,000 on field improvements.

By this time, it looked as though softball might recover from the strain it suffered from the war. According to the *1945 ASA Guide,* "There was a decrease of approximately

Opening night of the 1944 ASA World Championships in Lakewood, OH at Elks Stadium with a capacity crowd of more than 10,000.

DID YOU KNOW?

Industrial Softball

Softball at one time was the leading industrial sport in the United States. In fact, dating as far back as 1914, Eastman Kodak of Rochester, New York, would hold games for three leagues every lunch hour, Monday–Friday. Games started at 12:30 pm and lasted exactly thirty minutes. None of the teams wore uniforms, as there wasn't time for changing.

In 1944, Kodak launched its Kodak Park Athletic Association, which for many years was directed by Hall-of-Famer Harold "Shifty" Gears. When the program began, 860 boys aged 11–15 participated. By 1950, that figure had reached 2,640 boys in twenty-two leagues.

Kodak wasn't the only company in support of industrial softball. Grumman Aircraft of Long Island had as many as 1,000 employees playing in fifty-two leagues on ten fields. It was estimated that close to 200,000 spectators watched 1,050 of Grumman Aircraft's lunch-hour games. Frigidaire division of General Motors had 550 employees in its softball program in Dayton, Ohio. The Evandale plant of GE had 1,290. Chrysler Corporation had 394 teams in Detroit and eighty-four other teams in Chrysler plants in other cities. As many as 5,736 employees a week were participating in Chrysler's softball program. The Fort Wayne Zollner Pistons had a Knot Hole Gang for kids in the Fort Wayne area. And Dow Chemical, 1951 ASA national champion, had a Junior Dow AC program for youngsters in Midland, Michigan.

Besides the companies that sponsored softball for employees, there was the National Industrial Fastball League, which consisted of the top men's fast-pitch teams in the United States. The league changed names twice, however, and folded after 1954, the last year for the famed Fort Wayne Zollner Pistons.

18,000 service teams in the United States in 1944, but nearly 49,000 participated in the ASA program. The ASA assisted more than 1,200 schools with approximately 30,000 boys' and girls' teams in sponsoring softball during the year. The civilian teams numbered approximately 215,000, with the majority of them being in war plants."

The commissioners' meeting was held February 3–4, 1945, in New York City. At the meeting, it was decided that the job of secretary-treasurer would be split, making each position independent of each other. Although Pauley didn't attend the meeting, he approved the motion. Vice President Charles Foster was nominated for treasurer, but because of numerous other duties he declined and asked that his name be dropped from nomination and replaced with that of Gus I. Kern of Cleveland, Ohio.

During the meeting, the commissioners voted that each state association be charged an additional fifty dollars in addition to its regular $100 affiliation fee, and that each Metro association be charged an additional $100 plus its $100 affiliation fee. This was done to pay off the Association's debt of $10,330.85. At the meeting, the commissioners also voted to increase the dues of the International Federation of Umpires to $3, with a dollar going back to the Association to which the umpire was a member of and $2 going to the national office. The date of the annual meeting was changed to the last week in January or the first week in February and was to be held in the same city that was scheduled to host the Sporting Goods Dealers Convention.

In 1945 the ASA also approved an Industrial World's Championship Invitational Tournament, with an entry fee of $100. President Johnson named a committee of eight men to run the tournament, which was to allow no more than four teams from any state association and no more than two from any metro association. Seven teams eventually competed in the event, in which the Briggs Bombers defeated the Fort Wayne (Indiana) Zollner Pistons. The event realized $700 for the ASA national treasury.

Coca-Cola provided trophies that year to all tournament winners, including national, regional, state, metro, industrial, junior, high school and service. Johnson explained the program at the Spring Commissioners' Meeting on April 10, 1943, in Chicago, Illinois, at the Medinah Athletic Club and said that the Association wasn't to receive any money, but it (Coca-Cola) would purchase the softball awards for the ASA to present to civilian, U.S. Service Camp and high school intramural championships. All of these awards were to be presented by the affiliated associations of the ASA through their regular appointed commissioners.

Despite the war, and the unsettled conditions, the ASA enjoyed a most successful season in 1945, just as it did throughout the war years, wrote President Johnson in the *1946 ASA Guide.* The total number of teams in the U.S., Canada and Mexico that year was approximately 600,000, a figure that staggers the imagination of even those who had the foresight in 1933 to organize the game.

Coca-Cola's Chuck Swan, Kaliska's successor, attended the 1946 World Championships and also visited many of the commissioners throughout the year. If there was a problem with the Coca-Cola bottlers and the commissioners, it was a lack of communication between the two with each not knowing what was expected of them.

Swan said that "Coca-Cola was negligent in advising our bottlers on how the ASA was organized and it has been the purpose of my trip to get ASA commissioners and our bottlers acquainted and at the same time point out to the bottlers the tie-up advantage. In many cases, our bottlers didn't know such a thing existed as a Coca-Cola Softball Award. Therefore, some of you didn't get as full cooperation from the bottlers as expected—at least that is what I found." Swan upped Coca-Cola's contributions to $25,000 in 1947.

Byron Eugene Martin, Eastern vice president and Newark ASA commissioner, was elected national treasurer at the 1946 National Council Meeting with a budget of $22,839 approved by the Executive Board. Martin got seventeen votes to seven for Gus I. Kern, with five non-votes. Kern's salary as treasurer was $400 per year; Martin's new salary was $1,000 per year.

Executive Secretary Pauley did his work from two different locations. From May to November, he worked from Suite 901 of the Swetland Building in Cleveland, Ohio; while from November to May he worked from the Municipal Pier in Saint Petersburg, Florida. Pauley made all of the ASA's deposits and withdrawals until April 14, 1945.

With his duties at the newspaper increasing, Johnson, at the executive board meeting held January 16–18, 1948, in Houston's Rich Hotel, told commissioners that it would be impossible for him to again serve as president, and he asked that Walter Hakanson be nominated for president. Hakanson won the election, running against fellow nominee James Lang, and he succeeded Johnson on January 18, 1948. Lang later served as ASA president (1951–52). At the executive board meeting, seven commissioners resigned, and seven new ones took their place. W.W. (Bill) Kethan of Houston, Texas, replaced C.C.

Admiring trophies for the 1945 ASA Championships are (from left) M.J. Pauley, ASA executive secretary, W. T. Wood, Cleveland Coca-Cola bottler and Charles A. Foster, Cleveland Metro Commissioner.

Fred Zollner & the Pistons

Fred Zollner loved his team and loved to win. During the fifteen years he sponsored the famed Fort Wayne Zollner Pistons men's fast-pitch team, they compiled a record of 1,253 wins and only 189 losses, for a winning percentage of .869 against the best competition. And, in five ASA nationals, his team won twenty-four games and lost only five, winning three consecutive ASA national titles (1945–1947).

Zollner's desire to win is perhaps best reflected by his actions during a 1947 game against the Rochester Russers. During this game, Fort Wayne pitcher Elmer Rohrs, one of nine Pistons in the ASA National Softball Hall of Fame, had whiffed twenty-two consecutive batters when the twenty-third batter hit a long foul ball over the fence. Not willing to risk his team's winning percentage, Zollner immediately dispatched his four other pitchers to the bullpen to warm up. Rohrs survived the foul ball, however, and ended the game with twenty-five strikeouts.

There wasn't anything within reason Fred Zollner wouldn't do for his team, including building the $85,000 Zollner Softball Stadium. Construction was started January 12, 1946 and the stadium was opened on May 30, 1947.

In addition to his remarkable achievements in softball, Zollner is a member of the National Basketball Hall of Fame. He died on June 21, 1982, at age eighty-one.

Above: Fred Zollner.
Right: the Fort Wayne Zollner Stadium.

Cunningham, who recommended Kethan for the position. And Nick J. Barack replaced James Rhodes, who later became governor of Ohio. Kethan and Barack would play important roles in the eventual formation of the International Softball Federation, an association that helped softball earn worldwide acceptance and a spot in the 1996 Olympics.

Houston and Portland, Oregon, bid for the men's tournament that year, but Charles Foster deemed that the "bids were unnecessary because Cleveland ASA had an agreement with two more years to run." President Johnson asked "whether or not [Cleveland's agreement] was in contract form," but Foster said Jack O'Malia (the Elks Stadium manager) had a letter from Secretary Pauley. The president asked O'Malia if he had the letter with him. He said he didn't, and after much discussion Foster decreed that if another association could beat Cleveland's bid price, the ASA would cancel their agreement with Cleveland and go with the higher bidder. Metro Cleveland and Metro Houston eventually withdrew their bids, and Portland was awarded the 1948 World Championship.

Just prior to the 1949 annual meeting in Chicago on January 28, Pauley resigned as ASA executive secretary, ending sixteen years of service to the ASA. In his letter of resignation (dated January 27, 1949) Pauley wrote, "my health can no longer stand the rigors of conducting the office." Martin succeeded Pauley as executive secretary-treasurer, and would soon prove himself invaluable to the ASA and its progress.

A native of Kokomo, Indiana, Martin majored in commerce and finance at Indiana University and played basketball and football. He also promoted college basketball and boxing for four years at the National Guard Armory in Indianapolis. Martin served the ASA until his death on July 14, 1962. A victim of cancer, he was only fifty-six.

By 1949, the ASA had registered the most number of teams nationwide since its inception, according to President Barack in the *1950 ASA Guide*. "It is our belief that this record registration is proof enough that the ASA with its new amateur code has been accepted by all who are interested in softball," wrote Barack. Among the umpires was the first female umpire, Madeline P. Lortan of the Bronx, who registered in June of 1950. Barack noted that the umpire organization numbered in the "vicinity of 5,000 male arbiters."

That year, the ASA also decided to hold the Men's and Women's Fast-Pitch National Championships in separate locations. The women's tournament was held in Portland, Oregon, and the men's tournament in Little Rock, Arkansas, where the Tip Top Tailors captured the championship led by pitcher Charlie Justice, who in 1974 was elected to the ASA National Softball Hall of Fame. The

The renowned Fort Wayne Zollner Pistons men's fast-pitch team after winning a record third ASA national title in a row in 1947.

Arizona Ramblers captured the women's championship, with the teams dividing up a travel fund of $3,000.

But perhaps the best news that the ASA had in 1949 was that it had its largest unencumbered balance. This positive financial news prompted the commissioners at the Commissioners' Council in Louisville in January 1950 to establish a travel fund for teams. While at the meeting, they also adopted a new constitution and by-laws, and they approved the organization of national federations in various softball-playing countries. "From these national federations will come an International Softball Federation which will be the representative body of nations in the Olympic and Pan American competition," wrote President Barack in the *1950 ASA Official Guide*. "There is not much doubt that this plan will become a reality at an early date, and our boys and girls will have a privilege to represent their country in international competition."

Barack, representing the ASA at the September 13, 1950, meeting in Austin, Texas, was elected temporary president of the ISF. However, the ISF didn't make any progress until 1965, when the first ISF Women's World Fast-Pitch Championship was held in Australia, with five countries competing.

CHAPTER III

1950s

SLOW-PITCH BECOMES THE PEOPLE'S SPORT

With GIs returning home after the war and going to college under the GI Bill, the U.S. culture settled out of 1930s' and '40s' radicalism and into a more consistent way of life. Of the 16 million World War II veterans, 7.8 million used the GI Bill to attend college or get vocational training. Meanwhile, the U.S. had high rates of unionization, government social spending, and taxes, giving its people a better quality of life. This better overall quality of life in turn had a positive effect on sports, especially on the ASA, which expanded its promotion efforts nationally through its first National Softball Week in 1951. This was only one of numerous innovations by the ASA during this decade.

The 1950s for softball was a decade of innovation and maturity. The innovations included the realization of a youth program, the beginning of slow-pitch through what was called the World Tournament for Slow-pitch,

the inception of a Hall of Fame, the development of the annual All-Star Fast-Pitch Series (for both men and women), the holding of regional clinics and providing materials and personnel for clinics for the armed forces, and the first National Softball Interpretation Clinic for umpires (March 27–29 at the Henry Hudson Hotel in New York City).

That year, 1951, the ASA also decided to hold the Men's and Women's Fast-Pitch National Championships in Detroit to help celebrate the city's 250th anniversary. This was the first time since the inception of the Association that these two championships were held in the same city. In 1951, the ASA also conducted a general survey of softball, showing 65,210 registered teams and 978,150 players and 8,153 leagues. Ohio led in the number of registered and non-registered teams (5,023) and players (80,368). By now, people had more leisure time and greater general prosperity (an individual's average annual

Facing page: presentation of the 1957 ASA men's Slow-Pitch National Championship trophy in Toledo, OH to Gatliff Auto Sales, Newport, KY From left to right: Joe Gatliff, sponsor; Al Brausch, manager; and Charles Chuckovits, president of the Toledo Recreation Commission. (Wesley Otis Photo)

salary was $2,992), which resulted in more participants and fans for sports of all kinds.

While fast-pitch had been the game of choice for many since the ASA's inception, the organization made a major change to its championship program in 1953 by adding men's slow-pitch. Slow-pitch's appeal was that almost anyone could play regardless of ability. Slow-pitch had been gaining in popularity nationwide and all that was needed was an organization to expand it to the masses. The timing couldn't have been better for the ASA and the sport. Many of the ASA commissioners were entrenched in various parks and recreation departments nationwide, providing a built-in network from which slow-pitch could grow and become the people's sport.

In the April 1958 issue of *The Sporting Goods Dealer*, Martin wrote about slow-pitch's popularity: "The game has grown beyond expectations, so much so that recreation people are finding it almost impossible to furnish all of the facilities needed, and this to our surprise has not cut into the [fast-pitch] game.

"It would appear that [slow-pitch] has been a means for many to play a game that does not require all the skill and equipment needed for the faster version. However, [the players] do use many more balls and bats, due to the preponderance of hitting involved. It will mean a great deal to the sporting goods industry." Because slow-pitch grew in popularity, the ASA was forced to limit its championships to only regional champs and added an industrial division (1956) to go along with the open division (1953).

Above: Smith Barrier (left), NC commissioner; and Miss Southern Softball, Frances Gidney; present trophy to (from left) Eddie Feigner, Arno Lamb and John (Buster) Zeigler, members of the Miami A.I.S. Flyers, 1952 Southern Regional Champions. **Right:** opening ceremonies of the Men's 1952 National Championship in Stratford, CT.

Nick Frannicola

On February 4, 1951, New Jersey ASA Commissioner Nick Frannicola, one of the pioneers of the ASA, traveled on behalf of the ASA to Garmisch, Germany, for the second annual EUCOM softball-baseball coaches and officials clinic. Accompanying him on this trip was a distinguished bunch of baseball players, including Stan "The Man" Musial, Jim Konstanty, Frankie Frisch, Charlie Grimm, Steve O'Neill, Larry Goetz, Elmer Valo, Charley Berry, Gerry Coleman, and Dizzy Trout. The trip from Newark to Garmisch marked the first time Frannicola had been in a plane, and he certainly made the most of it.

"It didn't worry me a bit," said Nick, "but I was sure glad when we landed and I could step on the ground again." On the ground, Frannicola admitted he didn't know how the GIs would react to him, considering the noteworthy baseball players and officials in the group. "But once they saw that I knew a little about softball, they were the most attentive and willing bunch I've ever worked with. These fellows really wanted to learn the game."

In Garmisch, 400 American GIs and fifty members of the German Youth Association participated in the five-day clinic. These represented the various Army and Navy bases in Europe, a place where softball teams outranked baseball teams twenty to one at most

military installations. Frannicola's outstanding work helped to standardize the rules and interpretations made by the individual base or company commanders throughout Europe. Frannicola's work eliminated the disparity among the different interpretations.

Nick Frannicola passed away September 2, 1983, at age 73, and is a member of the ASA National Softball Hall of Fame. His son, Angelo, succeeded him as Newark ASA commissioner. It's the only father-son commissioner combination in the history of the ASA.

Nick Frannicola (right), one of the early pioneers of the ASA, gives a clinic at Headquarters Air Force.

The ASA happened to be the right organization at the right time, as slow-pitch in the ensuing years became the sport of the masses. The ASA eventually expanded its slow-pitch program to include men, women, and youth. The first Men's National Slow-pitch Championship was held in 1953, and in time the ASA added various divisions of play and, with them, more national championships. Cincinnati's Ray Ernst, a member of the ASA National Softball Hall of Fame and former

president and executive secretary of the Queen City Umpires Association, convinced Elmer Gerin, Cincinnati ASA commissioner, to hold a then-called World Softball Tournament in Cincinnati in 1953. Ernst, Gerin, William A. Moore, (Cincinnati recreation director), and John Deaver, former ASA president, comprised the tourney committee. Twelve teams competed in the inaugural tournament, won by Shields Contractors

Continued on page 42

Slow-Pitch Gains Popularity

Although slow-pitch was played in the 1933 World's Fair softball tournament, from which the ASA originated, fast-pitch was the choice of play for millions of players for many years. When the ASA added slow-pitch to its championship division of play in 1953, however, slow-pitch gradually increased in popularity eventually comprising 80 percent of the softball played in the ASA. With slow-pitch gaining in popularity, the ASA expanded its divisions of play and sanctioned more national championships.

Unlike the fast-pitch game, which could be dominated by a pitcher — and it was in the early days of the ASA until the pitching distance was increased — slow-pitch appealed to the masses because just about anyone could play. Today, people of all ages participate, and there's action and thrilling plays that follow one another like ducks swimming across a pond.

In its heyday, all across America, people of all sizes and shapes, and from all walks of life, were playing slow-pitch. Some played for exercise, some played

to burn off tension, some played for fun, and some played because it was a difficult habit to break. One player said the reason he played was that he "needed some other excuse for leaving work early and coming in late." He was also "too short for basketball, too klutzy for soccer and too tired for jogging."

The increasing popularity of slow-pitch, however, didn't help fast-pitch, which peaked in the 1950s, '60s, '70s, and '80s. Still, fast-pitch had pockets of the country, where the game was popular, and it's still played today in regions of the United States, as well as internationally in Canada, Japan, New Zealand, and other parts of the world.

In the past, teams often had three or four front-line pitchers, but with pitchers getting older and not being replaced, teams in some cases either disbanded or tried to get replacements, particularly younger pitchers. But, because of the lack of fast-pitch pitchers, the ASA and the International Softball Congress joined forces and started a men's pitcher development

One of the hotbeds of slow-pitch was Cleveland, OH, and certainly one of the favorites places to watch it was Morgana Park.

Members of Skip Athletic Club of Pittsburgh, PA, 1964 National Slow-Pitch Champions, celebrate their victory and hoist the national championship trophy.

program in 2007. By early 2008, thirty-eight pitchers had taken advantage of the free instruction offered by the ASA and the ISC.

To be instructed through the program, participants first submit a DVD of themselves pitching. The DVD is then reviewed by one of the two instructors, who respond with a detailed analysis and suggestions on adjustments needed and drills targeted to improve necessary skills. Videos may be submitted every thirty days, and all costs except for the mailing of the video are covered through a joint effort between the ASA and the ISC.

Any male resident of the U.S. age thirty or younger is encouraged to apply. There is no minimum age limit for the program, with the youngest player being age nine and more than half of the players involved being younger than eighteen. Skill level is also not a requirement. Anyone interested in pitching is encouraged to join the program. USA Junior National Team Assistant Coach Gary Mullican of Yorba Linda, California, and former USA National Team player Michael White are the instructors. Scott Standerfer is the program administrator and can be contacted at standerfer@mchsi.com

"This program has really grown in the last year but we are looking for more [players]," Standerfer said. "It is more than just developing pitchers for the national team, but really to continue to grow the sport and create teams that can compete in leagues all over the country. This is more for beginning level pitchers who just want to work to get better and really develop their skills."

Although men's fast-pitch probably won't ever again reach the popularity it enjoyed in earlier years, this program will at least give fast-pitch a chance to survive and develop or maintain teams throughout the United States. On the other hand, women's fast-pitch, especially in high schools and colleges, continues to gain popularity. In high schools, women's fast-pitch increased 70 percent from 1990 to 2006, with 373,448 participants in 14,968 schools. In the NCAA, women's fast-pitch also increased 70 percent, from 1990 to 2005, with 16,609 participants playing at 932 colleges and universities in 2005–06. According to the SGMA-sponsored research "Softball participation has been declining for at least twenty years. The losses have occurred in the slow-pitch form of the game as adult leagues have dissolved and youngsters stopped playing in sandlots, backyards and picnic groves."

Men's Slow-Pitch

The Amateur Softball Association added men's slow-pitch in 1953. At that time, the scores of the games in the national championship were relatively low in comparison to those of the 80s and beyond. Increased research and development brought about better products, especially bats and balls, and athletes improved as some trained year-round. These advances had presence on the ball field, where slow-pitch scores reached unheard-of totals, and homers flew over the fence at unimaginable speeds.

The first team to score 100 runs in a slow-pitch game was Howard's-Western Steer, of Denver, North Carolina. The team beat the Conover, North Carolina, All-Stars 104–5 on July 8th, 1986, hitting sixty-one homers and scoring forty runs in the sixth inning alone. Howard's Don Arndt smashed ten homers, eight of which were consecutive.

Arndt ranks among the greatest players in the history of slow-pitch and joins a group (of both super and major players) that includes: Mike "The Big Cat" Macenko, Bruce "The Bruiser" Meade, Rick "The Crusher" Scherr, Jeff Wallace, Charles Wright, Craig Elliott, Dirk Andorff, Rusty Bumgardner, Todd Joerling, Hank Garris, Jeff Hall, Bill Gatti, Doug Roberson, Ron Parnell, Brett Helmer, Cecil Whitehead, Jason Kendrick, Todd Martin, Ricky Huggins, Bert Smith, Ronnie Ford, Carl Rose, Britt Hightower, Rick Weiterman, Mike Nye, Jimmy Powers, Wendell Richard, Dick "The Rocket Man" Bartel, Stan Harvey,

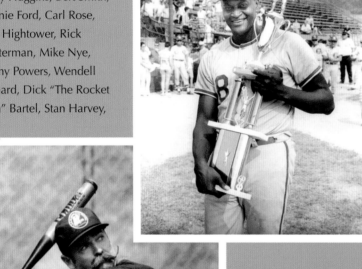

Dave Steffan, J.C. Phelps, Mike Shenk, Paul Drilling, Dewayne Nevitt, Jim Galloway, Andy Purcell, Dan Schuck, Darrell Beeler, Myron Reinhardt, Dal Beggs, Buddy Slater, Dennis Graser, Curtis Williams, Greg Fuhrman, Dewayne Frizzell, H.T. Waller, Denny Jones, Mike Cellura, Clyde Guy, Mike Gouin, Paul Tomasovich, Scott Brown, Scott Striebel, Larry Fredieu, Jim Fuller, Doug Brown, Joe Young, Lou Del Mastro, Bill Blake, Steve Loya, Randall Boone, Doug Kissane, Randy Kortokrax, Rick Wheeler, Dennis Rulli, Greg Whitlock, John McCraw, Monty Tucker, Tex Collins, Richard Wilborn, Shane Dubose, Greg Cannedy, Bill Cole, Tot Powers, Bryson Baker, Tom Beall, Russell Bradley, Steve Craven Don DeDonatis Jr., Walt Wherry, Mike Parrott, Phil Higgins, Mike Bolen, Howie Krause, John Mello, Scott Elliott, Greg Harding, Albert Davis, Chic Downing, Hal Wiggins, Rick Pinto, Herman Rathman, James Washington, Steve Williams, Don Clatterbough, Jim Mortl, Gene Fisher, and Bill Pollack.

Women's Slow-Pitch

The ASA approved women's slow-pitch in 1957, and held an invitational for the first five years. In 1961, eight years after putting men's slow-pitch on the championship calendar in 1953, the ASA added national championships for women, and ten teams competed in that first national in Covington, KY. In 2007, the Armed Forces captured top honors (four games to one) in a five-team field in an event at the ASA Hall of Fame Stadium held concurrently with the Men's Class A championship.

The number of teams participating in the championship has varied, with a record fifty-two teams in

Above left: the most recognizable slow-pitch player of his era, Bruce Meade.
Above right: one of the great slow-pitch stars of the 1950s and '60s, Jim Galloway.

Clockwise from top: Dana Gardens of Cincinnati, OH, after winning the ASA Women's Major Slow-Pitch Championship in 1962; members of Dana Garden, Cincinnati, OH, 1963 ASA National Champion, (from left) Karen Kuhnhein, Alberta Kohls, Dot Bailey and Norma Eschenbrenner Ante; UPI of Cookeville, TN, after winning ASA Women's Major Slow-Pitch National Title in 1992.

Parma, Ohio, in 1970 to fewer than five teams competing in the championship in the 1980s and 1990s. This decline was spurred by many factors, chief among them being lack of interest, by both sponsors and the general public (you rarely see pick-up games at the park these days); the trend of women opting to play for coed teams (introduced in 1987) over strictly women's teams; and efforts by colleges and universities to keep athletes tied up year round after Title IX.

Despite the decline in participants, there certainly hasn't been a shortage of outstanding teams and players. Some of the top teams include Dana Gardens, the Converse Dots, Marks Brothers Dots, Sweeney Chevrolet, Riverside Ford, Sorrento's Pizza, Bob Hoffman's Dots, Anoka Spooks (five-time champions), the Key Ford Mustangs, Cannan's Illusions, Tifton Tomboys, Richmond Stompers, UPI of Cookeville, Tennessee, the Lakerettes, the Rubi-Otts, Raney Tire, and Long Haul/Enough Said. Any of these could be expected to either win the national year or be among the contending teams. The top women's teams featured a band

of play that was endearing to their fans, featuring outstanding defense, solid hitting, and all-out hustle and effort.

Some of the top players include Donna Wolfe, Sherri Pickard, Carol Bemis, Kathy Riley, Brenda Smith Foster, Teresa Held, Linda Polley, Darby Cottle, Sandy Edwards, Tammy Williams, Cara Coughenour, Ida Jean "Hoppy" Hopkins, Alberta Kohls Sims, Norma Eschenbrenner Ante, Karen Krause, Nancy Oldham, Dot Bailey, Princess Carpenter, Sue Taylor, Kristy Boston, and Judy Hedgecock.

of Newport, Kentucky. In the years to follow, teams from Newport and Covington, Kentucky, and Cincinnati, Ohio, dominated men's slow-pitch by winning nine of the first eleven championships. The early style of play, which some called "Punch-and-Judy," emphasized defense, with teams getting hits in bunches, unlike the power game that later overtook slow-pitch.

After slow-pitch debuted in championship play in 1953, there were more teams than Cleveland alone could handle, so the ASA split men's slow-pitch into two divisions—open and industrial. By 1962, seventy-one teams competed in the two divisions. As slow-pitch's popularity increased, the ASA's team registrations also increased dramatically, and soon slow-pitch made up more than 80 percent of the ASA's registrations. To meet the ever-increasing needs of those wanting to play slow-pitch, the ASA increased its divisions of play, adding various national championships for men, women, and youth. They added the men's industrial division in 1957, women's slow-pitch in 1961, the sixteen-inch major in 1964, and Class-A men's slow-pitch in 1974.

Cincinnati, an early slow-pitch hotbed, hosted the first Women's Slow-Pitch National Championship over the 1961 Labor Day weekend. Most teams traveled to the tournament by car, with three exceptions: Interstate Life of Chattanooga, who traveled on the company's private airplane and had to make two trips to accommodate all twenty people in the group; the Milwaukee team, who chartered a bus; and the Aughinbaugh Canning Company, who chartered a deluxe coach on funds donated from Mississippi residents.

Chicago, softball's birthplace, eventually became the sixteen-inch capital of the United States. Although sixteen-inch popularity slowed down because of World War II and the Korean War, it regained momentum in the 1950s. In the ensuing years, the ASA would add more and more national championships until it had more than 100 national championships, with sixteen-inch added in 1964. Two men from the '50s, Tony Reibel and Al Maag, an avid sixteen-inch player out of Chicago, established the Chicago Sixteen-inch Hall of Fame in 1996.

As slow-pitch emerged into American culture, fast-pitch still remained very popular. The renowned Clearwater, Florida Bombers won the first of a record ten ASA national titles in 1950, defeating the defending champion Tip Top Tailors of Toronto, Canada, 1–0, in the championship game in Austin, Texas. The women's championship took place in San Antonio. It was the first year the ASA had implemented a travel fund to help teams attend these two championships. The fund helped thirty-three teams make it to the two

DID YOU KNOW?

Nicknames

With any amateur sport, especially softball, players have nicknames you can't forget, unless of course your team is on the short end of the score and you would just as soon forget the nickname. Rick "The Crusher" Scherr, Dick "The Rocket Man" Bartel, Ed "Fireball" Figelski, Norm "Cyclone" Warken, Harvey "The Horse" Sterkel, Al "The Horse" Lewis, Richard "The Texas Tornado" Willborn, and Mike "The Machine" Macenko are some that come to mind. Scherr, Bartel, Willborn, and Macenko all starred in slow-pitch. The others are all former fast-pitch standouts who starred as pitchers. Except for Warken and Figelski, all are members of the ASA National Softball Hall of Fame in Oklahoma City.

Facing page, top: Mike "The Machine" Macenko was among two players to have hit 6,000 or more homers during his career. **Facing page, bottom:** Dick "The Rocketman" Bartel earned ASA All-America honors six times and was a member of four national championships. **Left:** after another home run, Rick "The Crusher" Scherr receives "high-fives" from teammates assembled on third base foul line.

DID YOU KNOW?

Interesting Names

There were times when interesting names crossed the desk of former ASA Secretary-Treasurer B.E. Martin, who used the information in his column, "High, Wide and...".

For example, an umpire in Pratt, Kansas was named Cab Callaway (no relation to the big-band leader). Percy McConner of Pontiac, Michigan, is the only umpire in ASA history to hurl a perfect game, during the 1950 ASA National Championship in Austin, Texas. And last, but certainly not least, there was Wilbur Pancake of Columbus, Indiana, whom you can bet was probably a good man at the plate.

Also in 1956, the ASA, which held its twenty-fourth annual meeting in Newark, New Jersey, named Ray Ernst of Cincinnati, Ohio, to be the slow-pitch rules interpreter and assistant to UIC George Dickstein. The commissioners at that council also approved the establishment of the ASA Hall of Fame, to be run by its own special committee, headed by former North Carolina Commissioner Smith Barrier. Because of the success of the men's all-star series, women's teams around the country wrote the national office saying they, too, should have an all-star series. The commissioners' council approved the first women's series, which took place in Orange, California, in 1957. Together, both men's and women's all-star series generated publicity and boosted national interest, especially among the nation's youth.

By 1956, the ASA needed more space. Their lease was also about to expire, and a commercial company on the same floor needed the ASA's former office space. Fortunately, the ASA was able to get a rent concession on a larger and finer space for $420 less. Between 1953 and 1955, office rent was $1,482.00, increased to $1,599.72 for 1956. Byron Eugene Martin, whose salary was $8,000 in 1953 and $8,500 in 1954 and 1955, took a voluntary reduction in salary, to $8,230.52, to help cover the cost of insurance.

nationals, with $13,544.55 going to men's travel and $12,852.55 going to women's.

At the suggestion of Art Bauer, the Raybestos Company's coordinator of sports activities, the first Men's Fast-Pitch All-Star Series took place on July 14, 1956, in Stratford, Connecticut. Featured were the 1955 All-Americans and the national champion, Raybestos Cardinals, who played two in front of an overflow crowd of 7,256 onlookers. The event generated a profit of $540.80, which the ASA gave to the Boys Club of America to purchase equipment for youngsters.

Below left: Byron (Gene) Martin, sitting at his desk at the ASA National Office, which was located at 11 Hill Street, Suite 201, in Newark, NJ from 1949–1965.
Below right: reception room at the Hill Street office.

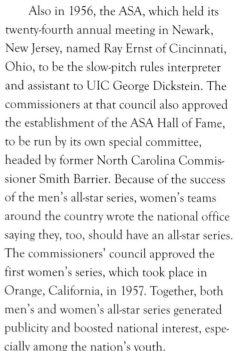

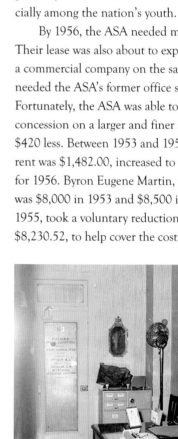

Mrs. Martin served as bookkeeper at no cost, saving the organization the $2,400.00 annual salary of a full-time bookkeeper.

In 1957, after a year of study, the ASA launched its youth program, which by 1959 involved more than 2,600 teams and more than 40,000 players. The ASA couldn't have picked a better time to start its youth program because at that time a staggering 70 million post-war baby-boomers were reaching the youth program's target age. 1957 also marked the ASA's silver anniversary, which they recognized by publishing that year's *ASA Guide* in a silver-covered front cover. Despite making changes and improvements to its programs, the ASA still operated out of the shoe box-sized headquarters (700 square feet) at 11 Hill Street, Suite 401, then Suite 201, in Newark, New Jersey.

1957 also saw the birth of the ASA National Softball Hall of Fame and Museum, and in that first year, four retired players out of fifteen candidates were selected for enshrinement. They were Harold "Shifty" Gears of Rochester, New York, Sam Elliott of Atlanta, Georgia, Amelita Peralta May Shelton of Phoenix, Arizona, and M. Marie

Wadlow of Peoria, Illinois. That year, Coca-Cola, which had been involved with the ASA since the '40s, announced that it would no longer be involved with the ASA in the promotion of softball, but would instead concentrate on more localized areas in need of promotion. In 1957, Coca-Cola spent an estimated $10,616.04 on ASA trophies and an additional $1,000.00 on promotion.

Above: Ohio Commissioner Nick Barack (left) presents Al Brausch with national championship trophy after his Joe Gatliff Auto team won the 1957 National Championship.
Below: Amelita Peralta May Shelton was an outstanding hitter as well as pitcher for the Phoenix Ramblers.

CHAPTER IV

1960s

OKLAHOMA CITY OR BUST

While the 1950s were conservative in nature, the '60s was a time of immense change in all areas of public and private life. The decade is often referred to as a social revolution global in scale. In his book, *Independents Day: Awakening the American Spirit*, Lou Dobbs called the '60s "a decade when citizens seriously considered what the nation's priorities were, and didn't like what they saw. For the first time our government adopted an 'us *vs.* them' mentality toward the populace, a sentiment that has reverberated far too strongly in recent administrations."

For the Amateur Softball Association, it also was a time of change, progress, and television exposure. Softball made it to television twice in 1961. ABC offered live coverage of the Men's Fast-Pitch All-Star Series games on *Wide World of Sports*. And on September 7, CBS also televised a taped coverage of one of the games in the Women's National Championship in Portland, Oregon.

In 1962, ABC tape-delayed the final game of the Men's Major Fast-Pitch National

Championship, played in Stratford, Connecticut. The game aired on *Wide World of Sports* on October 6th at 5 PM (EST). That year also marked a milestone for the development of softball internationally with the first Women's World Championship. Plans for the event, to be held in Melbourne, Australia, came out of the Women's National Fast-Pitch Championship in Stratford. Don Porter; Joe Barber, former ASA president and Connecticut commissioner, Jiro Iwano

Facing page: from 1966–1971, the ASA National Office was located at the Skirvin Plaza in Oklahoma City.
Left: a youthful and enthusiastic Don E. Porter in the New Jersey office after taking over for Byron (Eugene) Martin in 1963.

and Yoshitaka Ozaki of Japan, and Merle Short, Esther Deason and Marjorie Dwyer, all from Australia, attended a meeting to discuss formation and plans for the championship. The Australian delegation presented a plan for future international play and asked that Australia be considered the host for the inaugural event in 1965. The competing teams would be all-star teams rather than individual teams.

At the 30th annual national council meeting in Dallas, Texas, Fred J. Hoffman, Missouri commissioner, was elected president, succeeding George Cron. For the first time, the Hall of Fame Committee didn't elect anyone. As the work at Hill Street increased, the ASA Executive Committee met on January 24, 1962, at the Statler Hilton Hotel (Room 404) in Dallas, Texas, and discussed the hiring of additional help in the national office.

A committee of past presidents—Lou Canarelli, Fred Crosby, Fred Hoffman, Otto Smith, and John Deaver—was named to explore the possibility of hiring Martin an assistant. Nick Barack was named chairman of the committee. The committee recommended hiring Martin an assistant for $7,000 per year and giving the executive secretary a 10 percent raise. These expenses were to be offset by increasing the team registration fee from $2 to $3 and allocating $2,500 from television receipts. The committee felt an assistant would "be able to replace the executive secretary should the need arise." Little did the Executive Committee know that those words would come true months later, when Martin passed away.

Continued on page 53

Right: making the bid to have the ASA National Office and Hall of Fame located in Oklahoma City are (from left) Alvin Eggeling, assistant superintendent of recreation; Stanley Draper Jr., secretary of the All-Sports Association; Jack Moncrief, chairman of the All-Sports Association, and W.B. Auxier, Oklahoma ASA commissioner.
Below: Robbie Mulkey, batting in 1962 ASA National Championship, formerly held the record for most homers in a women's national (4 in 1949).

Joyce vs. Williams

The people of Waterbury, Connecticut, knew what they were doing when in August 1961 they arranged for Ted Williams, alias the Splendid Splinter, and ASA Hall-of-Famer Joan Joyce, now the head coach at Florida Atlantic, to play in an exhibition game to benefit the Jimmy Fund. Williams, who had retired from Major League Baseball in 1960, was forty-three years old. Joyce, an eight-year veteran with the famed perennial fast-pitch champion Raybestos Brakettes, was only twenty.

The exhibition was held at Municipal Stadium, which normally seats between 8,000 and 9,000 people. The crowd that day was more than twice that, with some fans sitting ten- to twelve-deep. Everyone attending knew that because both athletes were extreme competitors, neither one would give up.

Said Joyce, "He was a competitor, but I wasn't going to let up." Her pitching strategy was to keep the umpires out of it and pitch to an area where the batter didn't want to swing. She figured Williams' weakest area was up high in the strike zone. Williams fouled off three pitches after batting for ten to fifteen minutes.

Their second meeting, on August 5, 1966, was just a duplication of the first. Williams watched an outside pitch for a ball and missed three others. It was not the showing one would expect from someone who just a few weeks earlier had been inducted into the Baseball Hall of Fame. After striking out, with Joyce throwing nothing but rise balls, Williams went to the mound and hugged her, then waved to the crowd as he walked to

his convertible and drove away. In later years, Williams befriended Joyce and referred to her as a tremendous pitcher and as talented as anyone who ever played.

Williams (who suffered two strokes and died in 2002) and Joyce became friends.

Said Joyce, "We're very similar—competitive and proud. He loved to hit and test his skills against the best, and he wanted to be known as the best hitter who ever played the game.

"And, me, well, I just loved to pitch."

Above: another award for Joan Joyce, who played for the Orange, CA, Lionettes and the Raybestos Brakettes during her outstanding career.
Right: Hall-of-Famer John Spring showed Joan Joyce how to throw sling-shot earlier in her career and the results speak for themselves.

Insuring the Association

· ·

As the Amateur Softball Association continued to develop and expand its programs, for men as well as for women, the association realized a need to ensure the welfare of its athletes and umpires. In 1950, the ASA conducted a survey of the coverage offered by companies specializing in accident insurance. By 1951, the ASA finalized arrangements to obtain maximum coverage (group insurance for players and umpires) at minimum cost. The plan was designed and administrated by Yoffee and Beitman of Harrisburg, Pennsylvania, and underwritten by the American Casualty Company of Reading. In 1956, the insurance plan added coverage for age groups through the National Recreation Association.

Jim Bollinger, of Bollinger Insurance, noticing the ASA's continuing growth, hoped to convince the organization to have his firm handle the major part of its insurance program. Bollinger Insurance, conveniently enough, was located right around the corner from the ASA's 11 Hill Street address in Newark, New Jersey. By coincidence, the ASA and Bollinger were each founded in 1933.

So Jim Bollinger and employee (and son-in-law), Jack Windolf, who joined Bollinger in 1963 after spending four years in the Marine Corps, approached newly-named ASA Executive Secretary, Don E. Porter, and asked if they could make a proposal on the association's team, league, and umpire insurance for 1964. Porter agreed, and the two men made their proposal to the ASA Insurance Committee, headed by then Long Island ASA Commissioner, Dan Belcastro, who ran the committee with an iron fist. A buddy of Belcastro, Herb Schmidt, a deputy commissioner, was also deeply involved in the insurance committee.

Despite the Bollinger proposal's being "far, far superior" to the existing ASA insurance plan for teams, leagues and umpires, according to Windolf, the ASA had a deep-seated reluctance to change the present insurance program. Eventually the reluctance subsided and, with the help of ASA commissioners George Cron and W.W. (Bill) Kethan, the ASA finally accepted the proposal, naming Bollinger as the ASA's insurance broker for all lines of business beginning in 1964.

In time, the day-to-day operations were turned over to Windolf, who is the current chairman and CEO of Bollinger. In 1969, Jack and his wife, Muriel Bollinger Windolf, purchased the firm. In 1963, the firm, which had developed a reputation as a specialty insurance agency with a focus on accident insurance for students and athletes, had seven employees and total commission revenues of $200,000. In 2006, Bollinger reached a milestone of 460 employees and revenues topping the $100 million mark. It was ranked as the eighteenth largest insurance brokerage firm in the country in the July 2008 issue of *Best's Review* magazine. Employee ownership continues to be a major factor in Bollinger's continued growth and success.

Windolf, who attended forty-one consecutive ASA National Council meetings, has had his share of memorable moments spent with unforgettable people during his involvement with the ASA. One meeting he'll never forget happened November 9, 1965, in New York City, with former Boston ASA commissioner Jimmie Jones as committee chair.

Although demanding, according to Windolf, Jones was fair and reasonable and quite professional in chairing the committee. The meeting was held in the late afternoon prior to hosting the committee members for dinner at Keene's Chop House. Suddenly, in the middle of Bollinger's presentation, the lights went out—not just in the hotel but in all of New York City. It was the great Northeast Blackout of 1965, which stretched all the way into Canada. Jones postponed the meeting, to be concluded at another time.

Nick Frannicola, whom Windolf had crossed paths with years earlier, later succeeded Jones as insurance chairman. "The coincidence was that I had met Nick while I was in the Marine Corps coaching the softball team at the Air Station in Kaneohe, Hawaii," said Windolf. "I was informed that representatives of the ASA would be visiting to conduct a clinic for the coaches and players. Sure enough, heading the ASA delegation was Nick Frannicola. It was great to later reconnect with Nick and demonstrate how small the world is."

When Jacksonville, Florida hosted the 1966 ASA National Council meeting, Windolf, an avid golfer, took his wife and hoped for favorable weather so he could get in some rounds of golf, although the meeting was held in January. Unfortunately, there was a "real cold snap." The "temperatures hovered in the 30s for the entire meeting. I can remember that instead of going to a beach or a golf course, I took my wife to a movie to keep warm," recalled Windolf.

And when Orlando hosted the 1970 National Council meeting, Windolf and his wife invited Don and Jean Porter and Bill and Berneta Kethan out for dinner. "Insurance people like to entertain their clients as a way of expressing thanks for the business and to develop closer relationships," Windolf said. There was one hitch, however, or to be precise, two softball games, with one being late in the afternoon and one being at night.

"We ended up going to a Howard Johnson's Restaurant at 5 PM for a quick bite, then rushed back to the field for the next game," recalls Windolf.

"Over the years I've met some wonderful, dedicated people, and I got to see a lot of the country traveling to ASA meetings and conventions. ASA is my oldest business relationship and has been a meaningful part of our agency's business. Our staff has been proud to be there for forty-five of the ASA's seventy-five years. Congratulations ASA!"

Above: Bollinger Headquarters, Short Hills, NJ.
Right: Jack Windolf is Chairman and CEO of Bollinger Inc. He attended forty-one consecutive ASA National Council meetings.

Bertha Tickey

Known throughout her storied career as one who wouldn't back away from competition, legendary hurler and ASA National Softball Hall-of-Famer Bertha Tickey certainly wouldn't let an auto accident stop her from enjoying life. In November of 2007, Bertha was a passenger in a car driven by her friend when a truck hit them head-on at an intersection. Glass from a broken window cut Bertha's leg, resulting in her needing three pints of blood. "Luckily we were only three minutes from the hospital," said Bertha, who celebrated her eighty-fifth birthday in 2008.

While Bertha was in the hospital, she suffered a heart attack. "I didn't know I had one," Bertha said. "I asked the doctor if it was moderate or mild and he said it was mild. So I ended up spending five days in the hospital with three of them in intensive care."

During her stay, Bertha also learned that she had two blockages in one of her arteries, so she eventually had them cleaned out. "I had no qualms about that either," Bertha said. "My doctor said that my body was of a person ten years younger so I didn't worry."

Bertha had a career of almost three decades (1939–1968) that will not be matched, let alone surpassed. Playing for the Orange, California, Lionettes and the Raybestos Brakettes for thirteen years, Bertha won 757 games, lost only eighty-eight, and earned All-America honors nineteen times. She was a member of eleven national championship teams. Her career was filled with highlights and outstanding performances, including winning the ASA title for the first time. "That was in 1950 and the first one you always remember forever," said Bertha, who won sixty-five of

Pitcher Nancy Welborn (left) of the Orange Lionettes, receives the Bertha Tickey Award from Tickey herself. The award has been presented yearly since 1967 to the outstanding pitcher at the ASA Women's Major Fast-Pitch National Championship.

seventy-two games that season, striking out 795 batters in 513 innings.

In 1961, she fanned Baseball Hall-of-Famer Ted Williams in Connecticut. "He wasn't too happy about it," recalled Bertha. "He didn't say anything after it happened either. He invited me to a party later, but I didn't go."

During her career, Bertha also helped movie actress Lana Turner in one of her movies. "She was my favorite actress before I got to work with her," said Bertha. "But after working with her (showing her how to throw a softball) she wasn't."

Turner starred in the 1947 movie Cass Timberland with Spencer Tracy. "He was the catcher," said Tickey. The actress, who died in 1995 of throat cancer, was well known for the glamour and sensuality she brought to the screen, but led a stormy and colorful private life, having seven husbands and numerous lovers.

Tickey, who was married twice, met her second husband, Ed Tickey, while he was a catcher for the Raybestos Cardinals of Stratford, Connecticut. They married in 1963. Ed passed away in 1991. Bertha has a daughter, Janice Nelson, and three grandchildren.

Tickey's career brought her recognition in the media and appearances on various television shows, including To Tell the Truth and You Bet Your Life with Julius Groucho Marx, who Bertha said was "sharp as a tack." Bertha also appeared in Ripley's Believe It or Not. "I didn't think much of it at that time," said Bertha. "They called me from New York after I had pitched my 100th no-hitter. But I didn't want people to think I was a freakish type of person."

In April, 1962, Don E. Porter of Downey, California, joined the ASA staff as an administrative assistant. Porter, who had worked as a security supervisor for Chrysler Corporation in California and had been associated with softball since 1953, served as Southern California ASA commissioner since 1960. He was instrumental in forming the Western Softball Congress, which was a member of the International Softball Congress, a rival organization that catered only to men's fast-pitch.

After Martin's passing, the executive committee, while meeting in Newark on July 17, 1962, announced that Porter would remain as an administrative assistant and run the national office. They further announced that George Cron would continue to serve as advisor to the national office staff. Porter arrived in Newark on May 2. On May 1, 1963, Porter was named to succeed Martin, with Cron, former New Jersey and twelfth ASA president (1961), serving in a consulting role for the first year.

As Porter grew with the job, so did the ASA; in fact, the association moved its headquarters to Oklahoma City while he was in office in 1966. The late Einar W. Nelson, Minneapolis commissioner, was appointed by then-president Kethan as National Office Relocation Hall of Fame Chairman with the following committee members: Andy Pendergast, vice chairman; Charles L. McCord; Raymond Johnson; Eddie Moore; W.W. Kethan; and Porter, the executive secretary of the ASA.

Except for Porter, the remaining committee members are deceased. In a detailed four-part report issued on January 6, 1965, Nelson informed the committee members that relocating the headquarters was necessary; the space was needed and the bids were received. "The time to act is now, this year, when so many commissioners (110) and the executive board are in harmony

in acknowledging its desire for a National Office and Hall of Fame Building of its own," wrote Nelson.

The bids were presented to the commissioners at the ASA National Council meeting in Anaheim, California, held January 27–30, 1965. The committee's recommendation, by overwhelming majority (fifty-five of seventy-eight votes cast), was that the national office be moved to Oklahoma City. Oklahoma City won out over several cities: Stratford, Connecticut; Parma, Ohio; Clearwater, Florida; Richmond, Virginia; and Maume, Ohio. Nelson and the committee left no stone un-turned in finding a suitable location for softball's national governing body. The committee visited Oklahoma City twice, once before the decision was made and once afterwards. Correspondence between the ASA and the Oklahoma City Chamber of Commerce was extensive.

Kethan issued a bulletin on June 8, 1965, telling the commissioners that the national office would be moving to

Reception area at the ASA Office in Oklahoma City at the Skirvin Plaza, 1966–1971.

DID YOU KNOW?

1966 County Sports Team

Although the County Sports men's slow-pitch team of Long Island, New York, didn't win the 1966 ASA Men's Slow-Pitch National Championship in Parma, Ohio, they never envisioned that they would play eleven games in the last thirty-six hours of the tournament, and ultimately finish runner-up, with ten wins and two losses. The Jim Galloway-led County Sports ended up playing so many games in such a short time because rain on that Labor Day weekend tightened the championship's losers' bracket.

When the tournament opened on Friday, County Sports, in its initial year of slow-pitch, had the misfortune of drawing the defending champion, Skip Hogan Athletic Club of Pittsburgh, led by pitcher Louie Del Mastro. Hogan prevailed 13–5, sending County Sports into the losers' bracket. Before County played its next game, the rain started on Saturday and continued through noon Sunday, and when the weather cleared, the County Sports players knew they faced an almost impossible task—they needed to win ten consecutive games to make it into the championship round against Michael's Lounge of Detroit.

In order, County won those games 11–6, 20–8, 20–11, 10–9, 18–8, 16–11, 7–3, 20–14, 25–9, and 18–17 before facing Michael's at five AM Monday morning. In the ten-game win streak, County players hit forty-one homers with Galloway, who eventually was enshrined in the ASA National Softball Hall of Fame, hitting eleven of them. He finished with twelve homers and twenty-nine RBIs. Pitcher Bill Brown added seven homers.

Within forty-eight hours the County players had fewer than five hours' sleep and had spent thirty-one hours on the field. The fast pace proved too much for the players, who being (understandably) bone-tired, lost 10–0, getting only five hits to Michael's fourteen. After failing to win the championship in 1966, County Sports won its first ASA Men's Major Slow-Pitch National Title two years later, beating Jo's Pizza of Milton, Florida, 11–7 and 17–12.

Oklahoma City by November 15. On January 7, 1966, the ASA held an open house for its national office and headquarters, located in Suite 1351 of the Skirvin Tower, at Park Avenue and Broadway, in downtown Oklahoma City. The Skirvin was suitable for the time being, but the ASA needed a larger building, and eventually the headquarters was moved once again, to 4515 North Santa Fe, before deciding on a five-acre site that included the Oklahoma City Zoo, the Firefighters Museum, and the Omniplex science museum. The plot, located northeast of downtown Oklahoma City, was ideal for the ASA at that time, but as it expanded, the organization would need more than twenty-five acres. The national headquarters was expanded, as was the staff, which grew from four or five people to as many as thirty-five. With seasonal personnel, the staff can number as many as seventy people. As history has shown, the move to Oklahoma City proved to be one of the best decisions the ASA ever made.

In May 1967, UIC George Dickstein announced the newly created national deputy umpire-in-chief position, naming four men to the position: Tom Mason of Newark, Delaware; Frank Susor of Youngstown, Ohio; Paul Brown of Fridley, Minnesota; and Ron Derr of Portland, Oregon. Dickstein had previously served as New York City ASA commissioner before the pressure of being both the ASA UIC and the rules interpreter for the Joint Rules Committee forced him to resign. Dan Balcastro of Greenvale, Long Island, succeeded him as commissioner in 1954. Also, in 1953, Dickstein had compiled and edited a softball rules handbook for umpires and had held the first National Softball Umpires Interpretation Clinic.

Dickstein, who died Labor Day, had visited York a couple days earlier. Mason learned of Dickstein's passing while supervising the 1971 Men's Industrial Slow-Pitch Championship in York, Pennsylvania. He said that after the last game Dickstein asked him to go for a midnight breakfast, which Mason found unusual because Dickstein wasn't the type to fraternize with his

Continued on page 57

Aussie Women's Efforts Pay Off

Although the International Softball Federation originated in 1952, if it weren't for the Amateur Softball Association and three Australian women—Esther Deason, Merle Short and Marjorie Dwyer—the ISF would have remained nothing but initials on a piece of paper. While attending the ASA Women's Major Fast-Pitch National Championship in Stratford, Connecticut, in 1962, with nineteen teams competing from countries like Japan and Canada, the three women felt it was time for softball to have its own international world tournament. Within three years, with the support of ISF President W.W. (Bill) Kethan and ISF Secretary General Don E. Porter, the world tournament became a reality. Melbourne, Australia, hosted the first ISF Women's World Championship and ISF Congress. By 1965, fifty countries were playing softball, and five of them competed in the inaugural event, including the host team Australia, New Zealand, Japan, New Guinea, and the United States.

The USA, represented by the renowned Raybestos Brakettes, were the heavy favorites in the event. Unfortunately, they were surprised by the host Aussies, who won the championship 1–0, with the winning run scored on a wild pitch by USA hurler Donna Lopiano. Although it wasn't the start the USA had hoped for, it was the beginning of an era of exposure and growth for softball internationally. In 1966, the first Men's Fast-

Pitch World Championship (eleven countries) was held in Mexico City with the USA men, represented by the Aurora Sealmasters, of Aurora, Illinois, prevailing. The Sealmasters also repeated as world champions in 1968 in Oklahoma City.

By 1981, international softball had seen the first Junior Boys' and Girls' World Championships, followed by the first Men's World Slow-Pitch Championship in 1987, held in conjunction with softball's 100th anniversary. Modified-pitch was added to the international calendar of events in 1993, with Ponce, Puerto Rico, hosting the first men's and women's Modified-Pitch World Championships.

Throughout the development and the numerous World Championships, the ISF got most of its support from the ASA, whose national headquarters were in Oklahoma City. Porter was also the ASA executive director for thirty-five years before retiring in May of 1998 to devote his energies full-time to the ISF. Following his retirement from the ASA, Porter had ISF offices in Oklahoma City for a short time before deciding to permanently establish their world headquarters in Plant City, Florida, in 2000. The 16,000-square-foot facility is on seventy-six acres that also include Plant City Stadium and the Randy L. Larson Softball Fourplex. Plant City Stadium was built in 1987 and seats almost 7,000.

Aerial view of the International Softball Federation Headquarters in Plant City, FL.
Jeff Fay, Hollowtree Images

Pitchers Lead by Example

John Spring, Weldon Haney, and Al Lewis have something in common besides being members of the ASA National Softball Hall of Fame: each hurled a perfect game in the Men's Major Fast-Pitch National Championship.

In the finals of the 1958 nationals, Spring, of the Raybestos Cardinals of Stratford, Connecticut, beat fellow Hall-of-Famer Bobby Spell of the McDonald Scots of Lake Charles, Louisiana, 1–0, taking only sixty-two minutes and throwing sixty-seven pitches. In winning his fifth game of the tourney, Spring fanned twelve of the twenty-one batters, with only three balls hit out of the infield. In all, Spring fanned fifty-one batters in 26 2/3 innings. "It was fairly common in men's fast-pitch [to pitch a perfect game]," Spring said. But it certainly was not common in the finals of the tourney against another outstanding hurler such as Bobby Spell, who later in his career was Spring's teammate on the Raybestos team.

Haney, who died in 1989, was next to accomplish the feat, beating Oxnard,

Hall of Fame pitcher John Spring, when he played for the Raybestos Cardinals.

California, 1–0 in the finals of the 1968 National Championship in Clearwater, Florida.

Bill Currie of the Clearwater Sun newspaper called Haney's game "the greatest of his career." Besides fanning ten of the twenty-one batters he faced in the game, which took one hour and forty minutes, Haney scored the game's only run in the sixth inning after hitting a single through the middle and then scoring on a triple by his catcher, Al Varnum. Haney finished the tourney undefeated (4–0) and made a clean sweep of the various awards, leading in batting (.444), winning the MVP for the third time, having won it in 1962 and 1963, and being named as a first-team All-American.

Two years later, Lewis, who got pitching lessons from John Spring while working as the bat boy for the Raybestos Cardinals, hurled his perfect game, beating Salt Lake City, Utah, 5–0 in Clearwater, Florida. It was his only win of the tourney. The Cardinals became the third team to win back-to-back national tourneys. They also won the Atlantic Seaboard Major League title. Known for his grit and determination, Lewis lost the biggest battle of his career when he died of cancer May 23, 1994. He was only forty-nine.

Weldon Haney of the Clearwater, FL Bombers.

subordinates. Monday morning, Dickstein asked Mason's wife, Doris, to have a cup of coffee with him. Again, this was out of character for Dickstein, who met Mason at the ballpark Sunday morning and said he wasn't feeling well and decided to go home a day early. Mason felt that Dickstein knew the end was near. The next time Mason saw Dickstein was at his funeral a few days later.

The Northwest Region nominated Mason to replace Dickstein at the 1972 National Council meeting in Hawaii. Originally, twelve people were on the ballot to replace Dickstein. After three ballots, the final ballot was between Mason and Bernie Iassogna, assistant rules interpreter for the IJRCS. Because Dickstein held two positions, it worked out that Mason was elected national UIC, and Iassogna was elected rules interpreter. In 1973, Mason replaced Iassogna on the IJRCS as rules interpreter. Mason didn't want to lose a person of Bernie's quality, however, and he appointed him to his staff of national deputies, which included Susor, Brown, and Derr.

In 1967, softball was recognized by the IOC and was a demonstration sport in the Pan American Games in Winnipeg, Canada, with the Clearwater, Florida, Bombers and the Stratford, Connecticut, Raybestos Brakettes competing. The Bombers and Brakettes were each undefeated (3–0); the Bombers had defeated Molson's Brewers of Manitoba, 7–0, and the Brakettes blanked the Canadian champion, Fort Erie, Ontario, 6–0.

Furthermore, on the international side, Oklahoma City hosted the second ISF Men's World Fast-Pitch Championship from September 21–29, 1968. The winner of that championship was the Aurora, Illinois, Sealmasters. Ten countries competed, and delegates from twenty-one countries attended the event, held at All-Sports Stadium. It would be the twentieth consecutive year that the ASA operated in the black.

While the '60s saw the ASA increase in membership and six years of television appearances, the decade also marked the organizing of an active international softball body. Team membership likewise increased in the '60s, with 14,000 more teams and 5,000 more umpires. The largest team increase was 2,346 in 1969. Also by 1969, the youth registrations numbered 203,314 players, 12,377 teams, and 1,680 leagues.

The ASA was "the kind of organization that was needed to develop and promote softball as an international sport, worthy of Olympic recognition. This was not easy, but, through the diligence of a number of ASA commissioners and several foreign softball officials, amateur softball was given life and breath on a true international level," wrote Porter in the 1969 ASA Annual Report.

Carol Spanks prepares to round third, heading for home in the 1968 ASA Women's Major Fast-Pitch National Championship. Spanks earned first-team All-America shortstop honors as Orange, CA finished runner-up that year.

CHAPTER V

1970s

HALL OF FAME & HEADQUARTERS BECOME A REALITY

After the social activism of the 1960s, in which, according to Lou Dobbs, "our government wasn't interested in involving us in setting our nation's course," the 1970s shifted to social activities for one's own pleasure. The seventies were considered the "Me Decade," as people became more interested in themselves than in others. The ASA could point with pride to entering this decade, which proved to be one of outstanding growth and exposure for softball's NGB.

The 1970s also marked the death of Leo Fischer, one of the co-founders the ASA. On August 28, 1970, at age seventy-two, Fischer died of an apparent heart attack in a restaurant while attending a Shriner's convention in Atlanta, Georgia. Fischer had served as sports editor of the *Chicago American* for twenty-eight years, but he and M.J. Pauley are remembered most for bringing order and uniformity to the game of softball at a time

when it seemed impractical, with little chance of success.

Recalling those early years, Fischer said, "Gaining the public's confidence was the toughest task the ASA faced in those early times. The AAU fought us. So did recreation groups who thought we were trying to muscle in on them. Actually, the ASA as it turned

Above: Jiffy Club of Louisville, KY, Manager Bud Cagel (second from left), who led the team to the 1972 National Title. **Facing Page:** ASA President John Nagy bats during the ground breaking for the ASA Hall of Fame and National Office on December 19, 1970 in Oklahoma City.

Ty Stofflet
A Game to Remember
· · · · · · · · · · · · · · · · · · · ·

Ty Stofflet hurled thousands of games in his legendary career. But there is one that ranks above all of them. On February 4, 1976, in Lower Hutt, New Zealand, Stofflet and the late New Zealand star Kevin Herlihy went twenty innings, with Stofflet winning 1–0 in the ISF Men's World Fast-Pitch Championship.

In between the first and twentieth innings, the two pitchers combined for fifty-two strike-outs, with Stofflet fanning thirty-two and Herlihy twenty. The game saw only five hits, all coming off Herlihy. If he hadn't hit a batter with a pitch, Stofflet would have had a perfect game instead of a no-hitter.

Besides pitching the incredible no-hitter, Stofflet had two of the USA's five hits, and his two-out single in the top of the twentieth inning accounted for the game's only run. Although Stofflet said it was the greatest game he ever pitched, Herlihy had a different reaction. "To say it was the best game I ever pitched is debat-able. However, it is the one that I will remember more than any other. [The game] had been billed as the best left-hander in the world versus the best right-hander. I believe it lived up to and exceeded all expectations."

Herlihy sensed even before the game started that something special was going to happen. "What I remember most was the build-up immediately before the game," he said. "You could sense the huge home crowd had a sixth sense that something special was about to unfold. As the national anthem was played, I felt the hairs on the back of my neck rise. It was cer-tainly very special that such a game could be played in front of a hometown crowd."

It was the first and last time Stofflet and Herlihy would meet in ISF World competition. In the end,

neither Stofflet nor Herlihy would decide the outcome of the event. Mother Nature made that decision when monsoon-like weather forced the competition to a halt, and Canada, the USA, and New Zealand were declared tri-champions. That's the only time that has happened in men's ISF World play. It was an event to remember, and certainly the game between Stof-flet and Herlihy was the greatest game in ISF men's competition.

Left: Ty Stofflet uncorks a pitch in a game in 1984.
Below: Ty Stofflet was one of the stars at the 1978 National Sports Festival in Colorado Springs.

out gave tremendous impetus to recreational programs all over the world for we have always been eager to cooperate with recreation men. At any rate, the main idea was to convince the public that the ASA wasn't a racket of some kind."

On December 19, 1970, the ASA marked another milestone: the long-awaited ground breaking of the Hall of Fame and national headquarters. "The sun was shining and we're going ahead with the ball game," Don E. Porter said at the ground-breaking ceremony. More than 100 people attended the event, despite cold temperatures and chilly winds.

Other ASA people attending included the following: Kethan; then-ASA president John Nagy of Cleveland; Charles L. McCord, Illinois commissioner and Hall of Fame chairman; Hall-of-Famers Harold "Shifty" Gears of Rochester, New York, and Carolyn Thome Hart of Pekin, Illinois; Vince Ditta, Houston commissioner and southwest vice president; Ed Clott, Cincinnati commissioner; Andy Pendergast, Washington commissioner; Charles Boccia, Long Island commissioner; and many local and state officials. President Richard Nixon even sent the ASA a congratulatory telegram to honor the event.

Continued on page 65

Participants in the ground breaking for the ASA National Softball Hall of Fame and ASA Headquarters on December 19, 1970 included (from left to right) Hall-of-Famer Carolyn Thome Hart, Hall-of-Famer Harold (Shifty) Gears, Don E. Porter, ASA executive director, W.W. (Bill) Kethan, Texas commissioner and ISF president; John Nagy, ASA president and Cleveland commissioner, and Charles L. McCord, chairman of the ASA National Softball Hall of Fame Selection Committee and Illinois ASA commissioner.

The ASA and the Aluminum Bat

By Jess Heald
Batters Up USA Executive Director

Did you know the Amateur Softball Association played a vital role in launching the era of the aluminum bat? Well, if you didn't, here's how it goes …

Starting in the early 1900s, there were several efforts to produce a ball bat made from aluminum. These early bats were all doomed to failure because, until the aerospace industry emerged, the available aluminum alloys lacked sufficient strength to withstand ball impact and still be in an acceptable weight range. But after 1960, all that changed.

Before the invention of aluminum bats, wooden bats were in vogue.

During the '60s, as science developed stronger, more durable alloys, aluminum found its way into many sporting goods products (skis, ski poles, tennis racquets, snow shoes, racquetball racquets, pool cues, and archery arrows, to name a few). In 1968, Amerola Products, a Pittsburgh manufacturer of aluminum pool cues, used their cue-making equipment to fashion a softball bat from an aluminum tube. The bat was suitable for softball play only because it lacked sufficient strength to withstand an impact with a baseball. It had a maximum diameter of 2.0 inches, compared to that of most softball bats (of both then and today), which have the maximum allowable diameter of 2.25 inches. Amerola may have opted for the smaller size because a smaller diameter yields more strength or simply because a smaller bat weighs less.

Take a look at Figure A and notice the rather crude design of the end plug—a molded rubber plug held in place by metal rivets. Notice, too, the handle's distinctive wooden knob. The softball bat would not possess a more suitable metal knob for a few more years.

While this early bat proved suitable for softball play, it lacked one essential ingredient: official status for use in organized softball play. Throughout 1968, Tony Merola, owner of Amerola Products, had his bat tested for use in ASA play under the trademark Trucue—the same name used on Amerola's aluminum pool cues. At the January 1969 ASA Convention, the Merola bat became the first-ever official aluminum softball bat of the ASA. Soon after, it became the official bat of other softball associations as well. Legal status had been obtained, and the era of the aluminum bat had begun.

Subsequent to its official acceptance, the aluminum bat "gold rush" began. All the traditional wooden bat manufacturers, some aluminum companies, and a few upstarts centered development efforts on the opportunities offered by this emerging industry. The Easton Aluminum Co., which had developed the very successful aluminum archery arrows, quickly moved to the production of aluminum bats—first producing for other brands then for their own Easton brand. Another company, American Modern Metals, produced bats for several of the major brands in the bat industry for many years until these companies established their own production facilities. A new independent company by the name of Bombat produced one of the most popular softball bats for many years.

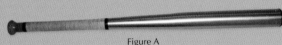

Figure A

One of the first official softball bats following the 1969 Trucue bat was the 1970 Worth softball bat (see Figure B). This bat featured a stronger aluminum alloy and a full 2.25-inch diameter. A rolled lip at the bat's end held the end plug in place, and the bat's molded rubber grip, containing a molded knob, replaced the traditional wooden knob.

From 1970 to 1975, the aluminum bat underwent many rapid developments as many companies entered the industry and competed aggressively for market share. For example, some companies began making bats with alloys strong enough to withstand the higher impact forces of hitting a baseball. Embracing these new developments, Little League approved aluminum bats in 1972, the NCAA approved them in 1974, and the High School Federation soon followed suit.

As aluminum bats made their way into baseball, an interesting old wives' tale developed surrounding the unique "ping" sound they create when striking a ball. Claiming that this sound made it harder for them to judge a ball's speed, infielders thought that a ball came off an aluminum bat faster than off a wood bat. But when they looked at how far the ball traveled in the outfield, they realized the hit distance was the same as expected for one hit with a wood bat. They concluded that a ball hit with an aluminum bat was faster in the infield but slower in the outfield. It wasn't very long before the players adjusted to the new sound, however, and the old wives' tale vanished into history.

The old saying "timing is everything" certainly applies to the rapid-growth era of the aluminum bat. During the 1970s and '80s, the slow-pitch softball game was exploding with participation, and the aluminum bat was just what the slow-pitch player wanted. Its increased durability and wide selection of available weights suited this new breed of softball player perfectly. During the '70s, in fact, most slow-pitch players preferred heavier bats, some as high as forty ounces. The Bombat brand became a favorite because of the heavier bats they offered. But the development of heavier bats soon led the ASA to implement another landmark action.

Concluding that heavier bats meant increased hit distances, the ASA in 1978 set a thirty-eight-ounce maximum weight limit on all bats—a standard that remains in the rule book today. Once again, the ASA had a "first" in the aluminum bat era. This was the first effort by a sports association to set a standard on bat performance. (It would be twenty more years before the modern-day performance standards were in place.) By 1985, however, the era of the heavy bat had passed as lighter bats became the norm. Today, a thirty-ounce bat is considered heavy.

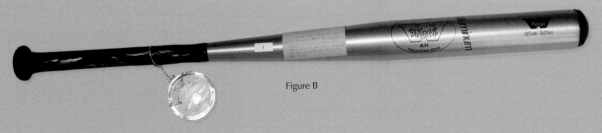

Figure B

An interesting paradox soon developed regarding bat weight between softball and baseball bat standards. The NCAA concluded that lighter-weight bats were leading to higher batted-ball speeds. In the 1990s, that organization set a minimum bat-weight standard.

Since the days of Abner Doubleday, the games of baseball and softball had been played with wooden bats only. But by the end of the '70s, the wood bat was a dinosaur, and the aluminum bat was the bat of choice for both softball and baseball. For the twenty-five years after its inception in 1969, aluminum bat technology changed rapidly, and those manufacturers who did not keep up were soon left behind. The company that started it all, Amerola Products, gave up production in the mid '70s. By then, all major brands in the baseball/softball industry were in the business and competing aggressively for market share.

The fast-paced technology brought new concerns about escalating bat performance. Higher-strength aluminum alloys seemed to be appearing almost annually, a development that allowed for bat structures of increasingly thinner walls, believed to be linked to potentially higher performance. The dynamics of bat performance was referred to as the "trampoline" effect, a layman's term for the elastic properties of the bat.

In 1992, a new specialty bat company, DiMarini, introduced an aluminum bat with two separate wall sections in the hitting area. That upgrade improved upon the trampoline effect of "single-wall" bats. The bat was very successful and, for the next several years, the other bat manufacturers scrambled to develop competing designs.

Then, in 1993, came the "ping" heard 'round the world. Two bat companies introduced a metal bat made from titanium tubing that added greatly to the trampoline effect. The wall thickness of these titanium bats was about 30 percent less than the strongest aluminum bat alloy on the market. But the sports associations yelled "Time-out!" and the industry spent the next several years developing performance standards to control batted-ball speeds and hit distances.

In the year 2000, the ASA introduced the first performance standard that set limits on batted-ball speed. Within the next two years, all associations in softball and baseball had some type of bat performance standard.

The "Wild West" days of the aluminum bat had come to an end. And, almost simultaneously, participation in slow-pitch softball decreased, a trend that began in the early '90s. Both the sport and the bat had grown up in the '70s and matured in the '90s, a thirty-year run of success for both.

Now you know the story of the ASA and the aluminum bat!

The author, Jess Heald, spent thirty-six years in the bat-and-ball industry, first with Worth Sports Co. and then with Rawlings/Worth, primarily in product development. Jess holds one of the early patents on aluminum bat design. He now serves as executive director of Batters Up USA, a non-profit organization promoting participation in youth recreational softball and baseball.

On June 1, 1971, the construction contract for the Hall of Fame was signed, and by May 2, 1972, the building (8,608 square feet) was completed. On May 26, 1973, the building was dedicated in front of an impressive invited delegation of ASA commissioners and Oklahoma City officials and dignitaries. Twenty-two members of the National Hall of Fame attended the ribbon-cutting ceremonies, conducted by Gears and ASA President Eddie Moore. Moore made welcoming remarks, as did Oklahoma City Mayor Patience Latting, Chamber of Commerce Manager Paul Strasbaugh, and Dedication Committee Members Fred Hoffman, Bill Kethan, John Nagy, Charles L. McCord, and Andy Pendergast. In conjunction with the dedication, the ASA also hosted the General Assembly of International Sports Federations (GAIF), held May 21–27, with people from thirty-seven international federations attending. And, even though the dedication took

place in May, the Hall of Fame didn't open to the public until July.

Wrote Porter in the 1973 annual report, "While the completion of the building project was a remarkable achievement in itself, considering that the ASA not too many years ago was finding it difficult keeping its head

Above: the ASA National Office operated at 4515 Santa Fe in Oklahoma City from 1971–1972, and was less than 10 minutes away from its present location at 2801 Northeast 50th Street.
Left: ASA staff members in 1972 included (from left to right) Don E. Porter, Sheri Hendley, Toma Malikoff (fourth from left) and Virgil Bowen (right). Hendley has retired. Bowen has passed away and Porter and Malikoff work for the ISF in Plant City, FL after retiring from the ASA in 1998.

Top: Hall of Fame building under construction, 1971–72. Bottom: an early picture of the ASA National Office at 2801 Northeast 50th Street in Oklahoma City.

above water on a year-to-year basis, the most important factor was its determination to be *the* leader, not only in the softball world, but also in the sports world in general." For a week, Oklahoma City was the sports capital of the world.

Tom Keller, GAIF president from Switzerland, said at the closing banquet, "We came to Oklahoma and found out what the real America is all about. We leave with a better understanding." Out of the GAIF conference came the formation of the United States Amateur Athletic Federation (UAAF), with Kethan as its elected chairman.

As expected, the ASA had an excellent year in registering teams and umpires in 1973, with 47,452 adult teams and 4,956 youth teams. This was the first time in ASA

history that combined team registration topped 50,000. Umpires increased from 17,252 in 1972 to 20,791 in 1973. The "big six" national championships were still held, along with seven additional national championships. That year, the National Softball Hall of Fame began accepting slow-pitch nominations for the first time.

In the 1970s and '80s, the Hall of Fame building was expanded twice: July 13, 1977, by 4,350 square feet, and July 1980, by 5,182 square feet. The ASA building and Hall of Fame now encompassed 18,140 square feet of space and cost about $1 million. Not counting the expansions, the cost of the Headquarters and Hall of Fame was $650,785, which was outlined in a memo to the Executive Committee on August 4, 1978, by Executive Director Porter.

"The long road to the successful completion of this important project was not easy, but through the perseverance, determination and faith of many of you and others, it became a reality," wrote Porter. "The building project has been an exciting era in the ASA's

Top: Don E. Porter, ASA executive director, Hall-of-Famer Harold "Shifty" Gears of Rochester, NY, and ASA President Eddie Moore cut the ribbon on May 26, 1973 to officially open the ASA National Softball Hall of Fame in Oklahoma City.
Center: ASA commissioners and former presidents representing 23 local associations attended the ASA National Softball Hall of Fame addition dedication in 1977 in Oklahoma City.
Left: Oklahoma City Mayor Patience Latting speaking at dedication ceremonies of ASA Hall of Fame and National Office in 1973.

Title IX: A Milestone

The passage of Title IX of the Education Amendments (now known as the Patsy T. Mink Equal Opportunity Education Act) on June 23, 1972, was a milestone in the history of women's athletics, especially softball. In 1973, the University of Miami, Florida, awarded the first athletic scholarships to women—a total of fifteen in golf, swimming, diving, and tennis.

But, as monumental as Title IX was, it proved to be somewhat of a detriment to the ASA because its women's leagues, which had thrived in the 1940s, '50s, and '60s, couldn't continue after colleges began offering scholarships. In essence, the scholarships granted a college coach the power to control a player's life throughout the school year. Furthermore, to stay on a scholarship, players who didn't want to play summer ball would have to attend summer school or participate in off-season training, effectively tying these players up year-round.

Two-time USA Olympian Dr. Dot Richardson

These stipulations were a contrast for those who played before college scholarships were offered, a time when players could freely focus on their teams and playing in a summer travel league in preparation for the ASA National Championship. But with the new demands of the college season, which required them to play sixty games or more, players in some cases didn't play summer ball because they needed a rest from the extremely competitive, intense college season. And with the popularity of college softball continuing to increase year by year—and

thanks to the excellent coverage of the sport by ESPN for helping to boost the interest—fewer and fewer women's teams are playing ASA Major Fast-Pitch.

Only the established teams (the Stratford Brakettes, for example) would be found at the Women's Major National. Little by little, those teams also folded, and the field of teams for the Women's Major decreased by at least half. The end result of Title IX's impact on the ASA is that it shifted the organization's focus on women's summer softball from its major program, made up largely of college-aged women, to its eighteen-and-under program.

Title IX is not all bad, however, and as a testament to the benefits the act has brought to women's sports, Dr. Dot Richardson, two-time member of the USA Olympic team, exemplified what it meant to her. Growing up in Orlando, Florida, Richardson as a ten-year-old had an exceptional arm and was noticed by a man who wanted her to play on a Little League baseball team. Little League didn't have girls' softball then. The guy told Dot, "We'll just cut your hair short and call you Bob." Richardson didn't figure that ball playing was only reserved for boys. Thanks to Title IX, which helped open the door for gender equality within the sport, the rest, as they say, is history. Richardson, now an orthopedic surgeon, hit the first homer in Olympic softball and hit another one to clinch the gold medal for the USA against China in a 3–1 win in 1996.

history and it would not have been possible without the support of all commissioners, past and present, who believed it could be done and saw to it that it was done."

In 1976, the ASA became the first amateur sports organization to be officially recognized by the American Revolution Bicentennial Administration and was given the distinction of becoming the first member of the National Bicentennial Sports Alliance. To honor this distinction, a special ASA-Bicentennial emblem was made. ASA registrations topped more than 82,000 adult and youth teams, and umpire registrations totaled 34,051.

With slow-pitch gaining in popularity throughout the United States, the ASA gave the sport another boost by holding the first

North American Slow-Pitch Championship (July 9–11, 1976) at Brookside Park in Cleveland. Pyramid Cafe of Cleveland (1975 ASA national champions) and Poindexter Lumber of Winston-Salem, North Carolina,

Above: early rotunda inside the ASA National Softball Hall of Fame in Oklahoma City.
Left: then Oklahoma Governor David Boren (left) cuts ribbon to officially open the ASA National Softball Hall of Fame and Museum addition on July 23, 1977. Assisting is Andy Pendergast, ASA president, of Bremerton, WA.

Diversity

Long before other softball organizations were formed, the Amateur Softball Association led the way in providing opportunities for men and women as well as youth. Although numerous other softball organizations have sprung up in the last forty-plus years, the ASA remains the leader in giving people of all ages, sizes, and shapes, from all economic backgrounds and cultures, the chance to play softball at nearly all levels of play.

As the national governing body of softball in the United States, the ASA takes that responsibility seriously and, when passing rules and regulations, strives to ensure fairness to all who play under its auspices. Before the ASA was formed in 1933, softball existed in a state of confusion, and the rules differed from state to state. Through the formation of the ASA, plus the work of the International Joint Rules Committee on Softball, the sport gained stability and consistency throughout the United States. And the different associations that the ASA formed and incorporated deserve thanks for their help as well. For example, the Texas ASA, which has been incorporated since 1952, has been one of the outstanding associations in the ASA for many years thanks to the untiring efforts of people like W.W. (Bill) Kethan and Jack Aaron, former ASA presidents, and Bill Williams, Ronnie Isham, and Glenn Morrison, the current Texas ASA commissioner.

While the associations' personnel has changed over time, the consistency, integrity, and fairness has not, and each year, more than three million people play ASA softball, a testament to the quality programs offered nationwide by the ASA's eighty-three local associations.

represented the ASA and the United States against two Canadian teams. Pyramid had won the ASA Slow-Pitch World Series against the Industrial champion, the Nassau County Police (1975 national champion), in a five-game sweep. One of the Canadian teams, Copain's, defeated Poindexter 12–5 in the championship game of the North American Slow-Pitch Championship.

While the ASA was gaining in stature, so was the sport, which was finally accepted into the 1979 Pan American program for San Juan, Puerto Rico. The USA women captured gold, beating Puerto Rico, 2–0, and the men earned a silver after losing a heart-breaking fourteen-inning, 1–0 decision to Canada in the championship game. In addition to its debut on the Pan American program, the ASA also had representation on the Board of Directors of the USOC for the first time.

On June 23, 1979, at the ASA national headquarters, the renowned "Play at Home" sculpture was dedicated to all softball players and umpires worldwide. Since its dedication, the sculpture by Leonard McMurry has become a favorite, with teams and individuals stopping to pose for pictures with it during their visits to the ASA National Softball Hall of Fame and Museum.

On October 22, 1979, the ASA reached another milestone as the 100,000th adult team registered. The team was one of 5,548 registered by the Ohio ASA, headed by

Continued on page 73

Facing page, left: Rocky Santilli (left), USA assistant coach, accepts congratulations from Bob Van Umpe, North American vice president of the ISF, at the 1979 Pan American Games in Puerto Rico after the USA lost 1–0 14 inning game to Canada in gold medal game. **Facing page, right:** the 1979 USA Men's National Team looks dejected after their loss to Canada.

Top: on June 23, 1979, the ASA dedicated the sculpture, "Play at Home," with among the attendees (from left to right) commissioners Andy Pendergast, Ferris Reid, Andy Loechner, Wayne Myers, W.W. (Bill) Kethan, Cliff Warrick, W.B. Auxier, C. Tillman Ryser, Harold Engelhardt, Desmond Roy and Carl Kelley. Kneeling are (from left to right) Andy Yazwinsi, O.W. (Bill) Smith and Charles L. McCord.

Bottom: after winning 1979 Pan American gold, USA team members in San Juan, Puerto Rico (from left to right), Linda Spagnolo, Barbara Reinalda and Julie Ann Winklepleck rejoice.

Bill Humphrey

. . . .

There isn't much Bill Humphrey hasn't done in softball. Player, umpire, umpire-in-chief, commissioner, ASA president, national office employee, one of the founders of the ASA National Umpire School, committee chair, and member of the ASA national umpire staff are some of the positions Humphrey has held during his fifty-nine-year love affair with softball. Some people might feel regret upon giving up one or all of these positions. And some people can't make decisions and sit on the branch before falling off. Not Humphrey. He's the kind who's always liked a challenge, and once he's set his mind on something, it's cast in stone.

That's the way he was in the late 1970s, when people discussed the possibility of the ASA having national umpire schools throughout the United States. The idea sat idle for quite some time, until Tom Mason, former ASA National Umpire-in-Chief (UIC), got together with Humphrey and Ron Jeffers of Cincinnati, Ohio, to make the ASA National Umpire Schools a reality. "We met in Cincinnati [Jeffers' hometown]," said Humphrey. "I believe it was in 1979 and we petitioned the ASA Board of Directors to allow us to have a trial school in Indianapolis."

Although the three were in favor of having the schools, the Board of Directors felt otherwise and turned down their proposal at the 1981 National Council meeting.

Bill Humphrey served as president of the ASA from 1997–98 and was instrumental with Tom Mason and Ron Jeffers in starting the ASA National Umpire Schools.

It felt as though the issue was dead forever until umpire committee chair G. Pat Adkison, former Alabama ASA commissioner and the only four-term ASA president, spoke to the board after their vote. Adkison, who has been an ASA umpire for forty-four years and has worked eleven ASA nationals, convinced the board to rule in favor of having the schools, including the proposed trial school in Indianapolis.

Some ninety umpires attended the Indianapolis school, and afterwards they filled out a survey, the overwhelming consensus of which was to continue holding the schools.

Initially, the ASA held five schools, and then they expanded to seven or eight schools so the ASA's fifteen regions would be done in a couple of years. "[The schools] set the tone for our training," Humphrey said. "They were extremely successful and ASA has trained thousands of umpires." That was a defining moment in Humphrey's career.

A few years earlier in 1978, Humphrey had another defining moment in his career, when the USOC held its first National Sports Festival (eventually renamed the U.S. Olympic Festival) in Colorado Springs. Before softball made its Olympic debut in 1996, the festival was one of a bevy of events the ASA could count on to showcase its best athletes (umpires included), get additional exposure for the sport, and help sell the outstanding skill level of the competing athletes. Tom Mason asked Humphrey to be one his umpires for the event. Humphrey worked the men's division, which consisted of the top four finishing teams from the 1977 ASA Men's Major Fast-Pitch National Championship. "It was a fantastic program not only for softball, but for all the sports involved," Humphrey said. "I wish we still had it."Although he was selected to umpire, earlier in his career, Humphrey, who played center field, had hoped to play for the Dow A.C.s, which was the premier men's fast-pitch team in Midland and winner of the 1951 ASA National Championship. But in a game against Hall of Fame hurler Bonnie Jones of Detroit, Humphrey, who faced Jones three times but didn't strike out, realized, "It was time for me to quit playing and start umpiring."

Apart from softball umpiring, Bill worked football and basketball during his career. But once named to the ASA National Umpire staff at age thirty-seven, he gave up the other sports. "It was a new challenge for me and I felt it needed more attention than continuing to do the other sports," Humphrey said.

Humphrey has made a difference in every position he's held in his softball career, and all of softball, especially umpires, have benefited. And his commitment hasn't gone unnoticed. Besides being a member of the ASA National Softball Hall of Fame and its Michigan Hall of Fame, in November of 2006, Humphrey was recognized in *Referee Magazine* when it selected fifty-two people who have been most influential in officiating history. The magazine also recognized two other former ASA umpires, Emily Alexander and Tom Mason.

Commissioner Howard Honaker (now retired). The ASA conducted a then-record twenty-three national championships that year and had record team and umpire registrations. The ASA finished the year with 102,111 adult teams and 15,583 youth teams. Events such as the adult and youth championships, the Pan American Games, the National Sports Festival, plus other events of note, were highlighted in the ASA's 1979 yearbook, which was also produced in 1980.

DID YOU KNOW?

. . . .

First Female Umpire

Madeline Patricia Lortan, a spunky, five-foot, three-inch, 150-pound woman from the Bronx, was the ASA's first female umpire, joining in June of 1950. She said that her being the only female among 5,000 umpires would encourage other females to give umpiring a try. "That'll kind of take the spotlight off me," said Lortan. "Right now I'm the only gal umpire among 5,000 in the ASA. Kind of awkward, isn't it? But I'm as good as any man, don't forget that."

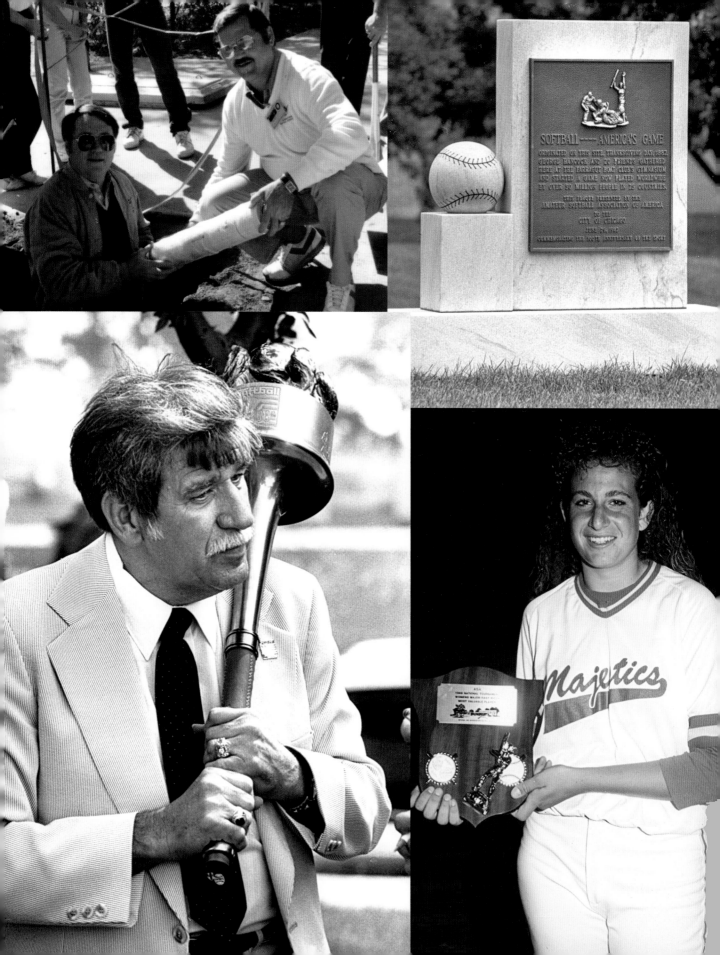

SOFTBALL ---- AMERICA'S GAME

ORIGINATED ON THIS SITE, THANKSGIVING DAY, 1887.
GEORGE HANCOCK AND 20 FRIENDS GATHERED
HERE AT THE FARRAGUT BOAT CLUB'S GYMNASIUM
AND STARTED A GAME NOW PLAYED WORLDWIDE
BY OVER 30 MILLION PEOPLE IN 75 COUNTRIES.

THIS PLAQUE PRESENTED TO THE
AMATEUR SOFTBALL ASSOCIATION OF AMERICA
TO THE
CITY OF CHICAGO
JUNE 2N, 1947
COMMEMORATING THE 100TH ANNIVERSARY OF THE SPORT

CHAPTER VI

1980s

SOFTBALL MARKS CENTENNIAL ANNIVERSARY

Although the 1980s were labeled the "Me! Me! Me!" generation, team sports for kids continued to gain in popularity from its inception in the '70s. The ASA was one of the organizations to benefit, taking advantage of the interest in youth sports by starting Junior Olympic Coaching Schools in 1983. The first five schools, introduced by former Georgia ASA Commissioner Bobby Simpson, saw 183 participants that year. By 1989, the program had eleven schools, attended by over 1,000 participants. From 1983 to 1993, the ASA's Junior Olympic program increased 130 percent, an increase due to a growing number of coaches and players, and to the work of Simpson and former ASA JO Director Cindy Bristow, who worked for the ASA for ten years.

The growth in the adult and JO programs brought an increase in umpire registrations as well, and the ASA made an historic move on January 1, 1980, when it

hired Merle O. Butler of Cupertino, California, as its first full-time director of umpires. Butler served the ASA twenty-five years and saw the ASA umpire program reach its all-time high—66,932 registered umpires in 1983. Between 1982 and 1986, the ASA registered in excess of 60,000 umpires each year. After retiring from the ASA, Butler became the UIC for the International Softball Federation, but on January 6, 2008, Butler died of a massive heart attack en route to the hospital in Edmond, Oklahoma. He was seventy-two years old.

The ASA, which had gotten limited TV exposure in the past, got a break in 1981 when Major League Baseball, marred by a bitter players' strike that lasted from June 12 to the end of July, cancelled 713 games, a third of the season. This allowed the ASA to get onto ESPN, which was looking for other sporting events to televise. The timing was perfect, because the ASA reached another

The Raybestos Brakettes

The Impossible Dream

If you know anything about the Raybestos/Stratford, Connecticut, Brakettes, you know they don't give up, even when the odds don't look that good. And in 1983, in Salt Lake City the odds didn't look good for the Brakettes winning their eighteenth ASA Women's Major Fast-Pitch National Title.

Their chances didn't look good because the tournament at the Cottonwood Complex had been shortened to four days, and the Brakettes were faced with the impossible task of winning nine games in forty-eight hours. That was after opening with a 3–0 win over Tuscon, then losing 1–0 to Sports Time Express of Sacramento, California, to drop into the losers' bracket. Brakettes' head coach Ralph Raymond kept telling his players "Nothing is impossible." The players made those words a reality by winning 7–3, 2–0, 2–0, 3–2 before capturing five wins on the final day of the tournament: 4–0, 8–1 12–3, 2–1, and 5–3 in the "if" (if needed) game against 1982 runner-up, the Sun City, Arizona, Saints. The Brakettes finished with a record ten wins and one loss. Brakette shortstop Pat Dufficy, named tourney MVP, batted .484, going thirteen for twenty-eight with eight RBIs. Pitcher Barb Reinalda went 6–0 and Kathy Arendsen went 4–1. Brakette Pat Guenzler, who went sixteen for twenty-nine, led the tourney in batting (.552) and drove in the two runs in the 2–1 first game of the championship round to force the "if" game.

Record-Breaking 1992 Championship

When the First Page Metros of Washington, D.C., played the Raybestos Brakettes on August 11, 1992, in second-round action of the ASA Women's Major Fast-Pitch National Championship, they never could have imagined the outcome. It was a contest that the Brakettes won 30–0, setting twelve national championship records, including most runs in one inning, twelve in the bottom of the first; most batters in an inning, seventeen; most home runs in an inning, three; most team RBIs, twenty-six; most runs in one game, thirty; most RBIs by one player, Dionna Harris, seven; most homers, five; most home hits by one player, Tricia

Scoring a run is Hall of Fame catcher Rosemary ("Micki") Stratton, who was the first of 19 Raybestos Brakettes elected to the ASA National Softball Hall of Fame. She earned All-America laurels seven times.

Popowski, five for five at-bats; largest margin of victory, 30–0; and most hits in a game, twenty-six. The Brakettes went on to win the national title, their third consecutive title and twenty-third overall.

Top left: 1981 Hall of Fame inductee Harvey Sterkel was one of the outstanding sling-shot pitchers of all time.
Top right: the ASA held its first formal Hall of Fame induction on June 20, 1981 at the Skirvin Plaza Hotel in downtown OKC. The inductees pictured are (from left to right) Shirley Topley; Carol Spanks; Billy Parker; George Adam; Dr. Margaret Dobson, who was inducted in 1964; and Harvey Sterkel.
Bottom left: Shirley Topley of the Orange, CA Lionettes takes a close pitch in the 1969 ASA National Championship.
Bottom right: ASA President Howard Honaker speaks at opening ceremonies of first Hall of Fame Classic in Oklahoma City on June 20, 1981 with Hall of Fame inductees behind him at Eggeling Stadium in Wheeler Park.

contest; games featuring the National Slow-Pitch Champion Rubi-Otts of Graham, North Carolina, against the Women's Major Slow-Pitch All-Americans; and the induction of Hall-of-Famers Harvey Sterkel, Carol Spanks, Shirley Topley, George Adam, and Bill Parker, all former fast-pitch standouts.

In the past, the ASA had inducted its Hall-of-Famers at selected national championships, but it took a giant step for softball with the first formal induction ceremonies. Among the special guests of Natural Light were former baseball greats Lou Brock and Mickey Mantle, who was born in Commerce, Oklahoma. Having Mantle and Brock there

milestone on June 20, 1981, with its first formal Hall of Fame induction with the Hall of Fame Classic. Sponsored by Natural Light, this first Hall of Fame Classic actually included four events: a fast-pitch game between the Oklahoma City Jets girls' team versus China; a national home run-hitting

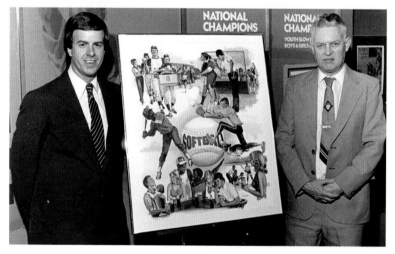

of course helped to generate considerable publicity and exposure for the event.

Although the ASA realized four events were too many, the game between the Oklahoma City Purple Power and the Chinese team drew 3,378 people to Eggeling Stadium at Wheeler Park. The crowd was at that time the largest for a softball game in Oklahoma City. ESPN filmed the home run-hitting contest and both exhibition games. The home run contest was replayed July 13, 14, and 17, and the exhibition games were replayed July 6 and July 8.

The Hall of Fame induction wasn't the only ASA event that got TV coverage in the '80s, however. With the help of R.J. Reynolds, the ASA put together the Winston-ASA Slow-Pitch All-Star Series, featuring the 1981 All-Americans against Super Division champion, Howard's-Western Steer of Denver, North Carolina. It was a success on and off the field, with the third game of the five-game series shown on the weekly show, *Sports America*, by 182 television stations during the third week of November 1982. The Winston-ASA Slow-Pitch All-Star Series was held the following year (1983) at All Sports Stadium in Oklahoma City, July 15–16. That year, R.J. Reynolds also provided trophies for all ASA state, metro, regional, and national competition. Because of the first Hall of

Top: discussing the first Hall of Fame Classic in 1981 are (from left) Patience Latting, Oklahoma City mayor; Don E. Porter, ASA executive director; ASA President Howard Honaker and George Nigh, governor of OK.
Center: Robert F. Merz (left), senior product manager for Natural Light, and ASA President Howard Honaker at ASA Headquarters discussing Natural Light's sponsorship of the first National Softball Hall of Fame Classic.

Arendsen Fans Jackson

ASA Softball Hall-of-Famer Kathy Arendsen was always helpful and did much to gain nation-wide notoriety and publicity for softball during her outstanding career, which ended in 1992. In 1981, during the National Sports Festival in Syracuse, New York, Arendsen took the mound for a little pitching experiment against New York Yankee Reggie Jackson, who was in town covering the NSF for ABC's *Wide World of Sports*.

Jackson never saw the ball, as Arendsen fanned him three straight times as the highlight of a rainy afternoon at Syracuse's Meachem Field, in the upstate city's north side.

"Reggie caught me first to see how I threw," Arendsen told the *Tulsa World*. "Softball pitchers throw from 40 feet [since changed] and under-hand. He still was Mr. October back then and in his prime. I worked him over with different pitches and never got to a full count.

"He was very complimentary and great about it. The publicity he gave our sport was amazing. He was impressed and told me I was as fast as major league pitchers."

"She sure is some athlete," said the humbled Jackson of the six-foot-two Arendsen, who was the first softball player to be a finalist for the James E. Sullivan Award, which recognizes the top amateur athlete in the United States.

In 1978, legendary left-hander Ty Stofflet, also a member of the ASA National Softball Hall of Fame, while appearing on a live Dick Clark network TV special, struck out Davey Lopes and Reggie Smith of the Los Angeles Dodgers, and induced Steve Garvey into an infield dribble in a special confrontation.

Kathy Arendsen, former Raybestos Brakette, was a standout hurler for the USA in Pan American Games and ISF World Championship play.

Fame Classic's success, it set the tone for future Hall of Fame weekends, which peaked in 1987 with the building of the ASA Don E. Porter Hall of Fame Stadium.

The ASA JO program—which had a record-breaking year in 1982 with more than 22,000 teams and more than 440,000 participants—got its first national sponsor when Wilson Sporting Goods of Chicago, Illinois, footed the bill for the program in 1983. Coca-Cola agreed to sponsor the JO awards at the regional and national levels.

At the ASA National Council Meeting in San Antonio, Texas, January 18–22, 1982,

Facing page, bottom: Baseball Hall-of-Famer Mickey Mantle signs an autograph for an admiring fan with ASA President Arnold (Red) Halpern (left) and Raymond Johnson (right) looking on during the first formal ASA National Softball Hall of Fame induction ceremonies.

OKC: The Mecca of Softball

Omaha, Nebraska, is revered as the mecca of college baseball. Williamsport, Pennsylvania, is revered as the mecca of Little League baseball. Oklahoma City has become the mecca of softball in the United States. This is due to the dedicated efforts, time, and money of the Amateur Softball Association, the sport's National Governing Body.

When the ASA completed its Hall of Fame Stadium in 1987, it probably wasn't with the goal of having the venue become a mecca. But as the stadium grew from having two fields (in addition to the main field, there was a back diamond) to having four fields, with plans for three or four additional fields and four million dollars worth of additional renovations, it appears the venue is destined to become just that. The renovations will include a new press box, an umpire-team meeting room, and a spectacular state-of-the-art scoreboard.

The renovations being made are intended to enhance the Women's College World Series, an event the ASA has hosted every year since 1990 (except for in 1996, when the event took place in Atlanta, Georgia, as part of an effort to generate interest in Olympic softball). With these renovations, plus the improvements the ASA makes year after year, OKC has become the mecca of softball.

The ASA Hall of Fame Stadium has reached mecca status because it hasn't just held the NCAA College World Series. It has hosted numerous other events, both international (World Cup, Tri-Nation Series) and domestic (Hooters USA Championship Series, Hall of Fame qualifiers, JO Gold National Championship, Oklahoma High School State Championships, USA National Team), with events booked for twenty-six weekends each year.

Together, these events attract in excess of 500 teams and 120,000 fans to the stadium, making it a busy, around-the-clock operation from mid-March to mid-October. An outstanding grounds crew keeps the four ASA fields immaculate despite the demanding schedule from March to October. The administration for all of the events is handled and coordinated through the ASA national office. The national office ensures that teams and coaches enjoy their visit to the mecca of softball in the U.S.A.

It's well worth the experience to attend this marvelous stadium, and it feels even better if you finish first in a tournament or win the NCAA College World Series there. It doesn't get any better than that in the world of softball.

Overhead view of the ASA Hall of Fame Stadium in Oklahoma City, which opened in 1987.

the ASA marked its golden anniversary and elected Arnold "Red" Halpern of Idaho as its newest president. The National Sports Festival—eventually renamed the U.S. Olympic Festival—was held in Colorado Springs, Colorado, with softball's Kathy Arendsen and gymnast Scott Johnson serving as the torch-bearers for the opening ceremonies June 24, 1983, in Falcon Stadium. It was the first time a softball player was one of the torch-bearers.

On February 12, 1984, one of the pioneers of the ASA, Fred Hoffman, passed away at age eighty-three in St. Joseph, Missouri. He was involved with the ASA for fifty years, serving as president from 1962 to 1963 and as commissioner of the Missouri ASA from 1933 to the time of his death.

At the 1985 National Council Meeting in Corpus Christi, ASA President Charles L. McCord of Illinois announced, "We will seek out and explore all avenues and possibilities to make Softball '87 a celebration that will leave a special feeling with all of us who are close to the game and for all persons, worldwide, who also play and enjoy this great game. While we are still two years away, much will need to be done in preparation and arranging a meaningful and appropriate Centennial celebration." McCord named a Centennial Committee that included chairman Andy Loechner of Pennsylvania and members Bobby Simpson of Georgia (vice chairman), Jack Aaron, Orie Chandler, Walt Cohen, Perry Coonce, Mike Engan, Steve Ducoff, Arnold "Red" Halpern, Howard Honaker, Elliott Smith, Keith Sandvold, Rose Stinson, H. Franklin Taylor III, Matt Urban, Bert Weeks, A.C. Williams, and Bill Wooten.

McCord was elected as president for a second year at the fifty-third ASA National Council Meeting (January 20–25) in Corpus Christi, Texas, which featured USOC President-elect Jack Kelly as the featured speaker at the awards luncheon. It also was announced

DID YOU KNOW?

Top Softball Leagues

The games are only memories, as are the various fast-pitch men's and women's leagues that at one time dotted the U.S. landscape. There was the Atlantic Seaboard Major Softball League, with teams located in several cities: Worcester, Massachusetts; Stratford, Connecticut; Providence, Rhode Island; Jones Beach, Levittown, and Huntington, New York; Elizabeth and Paterson, New Jersey; and Scranton, Pennsylvania

Another top men's league was the Southern Major League, consisting of some of the top men's teams from the South, including the Clearwater, Florida, Bombers, ten-time ASA national champions, and Combustion Engineer of Chattanooga, Tennessee.

One of the strongest women's leagues was the Western States Girls Softball League, formed in 1946 by Ford Hoffman, Erv Lind, Dennis Murphy and Shorty Hill. The league was later renamed in 1951. The best women's fast-pitch teams played in the league, including the Orange Lionettes, Fresno Rockets, Huntington Park Blues, Whittier Gold Sox, Portland Pennants, A-1 Queens, Sun City Saints, San Diego, Seattle, and Vancouver.

that two meetings would be held in 1986, one in January in Baltimore and another in Hawaii in November. The National Council also increased by fifteen with the addition of fifteen regional umpire-in-chiefs, effective 1986, and the first men's master's division (thirty-five-and-over) was announced for national championship play following two years of invitational play in Bloomington, Minnesota, drawing twenty-three and thirty teams in 1983 and 1984.

The ground breaking for the Hall of Fame Stadium was held June 14–15, 1985, in conjunction with the induction of four new members of the ASA National Softball Hall of Fame: Sharron Backus, Jim Galloway, E. Louise Albrecht, and Willie Roze. Twenty-four commissioners were among the 200 or so people who attended the June 15th

Right: Hall-of-Famer Harvey Sterkel starts the 1987 Softball Centennial Torch Run in Chicago, at the site of softball's invention.
Below: discussing the dedication of the monument in Chicago recognizing the 100th Anniversary of the sport are (from left to right), Don Porter, ASA executive director; ASA President and Pennsylvania ASA Commissioner Andy Loechner; and the Mayor of Chicago, Harold Washington.

ground breaking. Games involving national champion men's and women's slow-pitch teams were held at Eggeling Stadium in Oklahoma City. "It's an honor for me to be here and taking part in the ribbon cutting," McCord said. "It's a great honor for [ASA] and Oklahoma City to get world recognition. Some costs from construction are being paid for by donations from other countries.

"If you have a stadium like this, there is a definite possibility of hosting many things. There has been some interest in the Big Eight holding its tournament here—there's no contract, but it has been discussed. Oklahoma City is the possible site for the College World Series."

"We are going to have a lot of events here," ASA Executive Director Don Porter said at the ground breaking. "National events, international events...there are lots of teams and coaches interested in the activity who will use the facilities. Along with baseball, we are going to try to get softball to be a gold-medal sport in the Olympics. This could be used for training here."

Porter was correct about "a lot of events" being held at the Hall of Fame Stadium. In years to come, some of the most prestigious events in softball were held at the stadium, which now seats more than 5,000 people. Some of the events which, for all practical reasons, have found a "home" in Oklahoma City are the NCAA College World Series, NAIA Championship, the Hooters

Championship Series, Hall of Fame qualifiers, the World Cup of Softball, Oklahoma state high school fast-pitch and slow-pitch championships, and various other events.

In 1987, softball marked its 100th anniversary with various special events. One such event was the ISF Junior Girls' World Championship. It was hoped that the Hall of Fame Stadium could be completed in time to host the event. Unfortunately, it wasn't because of heavy rains in May, and the fast-pitch championship was held instead at Eggeling Stadium in downtown Oklahoma City. The event drew in excess of 50,000 people—the largest attended softball event in Oklahoma City history.

Besides the world championship, which was won by the USA, who featured teen-age pitching sensation Michele Granger (now a mother of four and a 2006 inductee into the ASA National Softball Hall of Fame) the ASA held a nationwide Centennial torch run from the birthplace of softball, Chicago, Illinois, to Oklahoma City. The run took place June 29–July 10, 1987.

In conjunction with the run, on June 29, 1987, a monument was unveiled and dedicated at the former site of the Farragut Boat Club (now Michael Reese Hospital, at 30th Street and Lake Park Avenue) in Chicago. Among those making remarks at the unveiling were Softball Centennial chairperson O.W. "Bill" Smith, ASA President Andrew S. Loechner, Jr., of Pennsylvania, and Chicago Mayor Harold Washington. They were among about fifty people who attended the unveiling, which kicked off the Marathon Torch Run, with sixteen-inch Hall-of-Famer Eddie Zolna (Chicago's Mr. Z) first passing the torch to Hall of Fame fast-pitch pitcher Harvey Sterkel.

From Chicago, the torch went through Blue Island, East Peoria, Pekin, Decatur, Normal, and Bloomington, Illinois; St. Louis, Columbia, Rolla, Springfield, and Joplin,

Above: John Brooks, former voice of the Oklahoma Sooners, welcomes Hall-of-Famers Nina Norgan and John Baker into Eggeling Stadium in 1987 to complete the Centennial Torch run prior to the ISF World Championship. Brooks also did a masterful job as the MC for the first formal Hall of Fame induction in 1981.
Left: former Tulsa ASA Commissioner C. Tillman Ryser, who served as director of the Centennial Run during 1987, puts the torch in place at the ISF Junior World Championship in Oklahoma City after completion of the run.

Missouri; Dewey, Bartlesville, Broken Arrow, Pryor, Tulsa, and Sand Springs, Oklahoma. The run reached Oklahoma City in time for the opening ceremonies of the ISF Junior Girls' World Fast-Pitch Championship, July 10, 1987. Dr. Nilda Reyes of Tulsa was the National Run Coordinator, former Tulsa Commissioner C. Tillman Ryser the National Run Director, and Madeline K. Gilmore the Centennial Torch driver. To help promote and publicize the Centennial celebration, a

Tom Wagner

. . . .

If men's fast-pitch was as competitive today as it was in the '60s, '70s, and '80s, Tom Wagner probably would still be involved in the game. "It would have been tough to quit. I would have remained involved in same way," Wagner said.

While he was involved, Wagner managed Pay 'n Pak and Peterbilt Western of Seattle, Washington, to five ASA national titles (1979–1988. In 1987, he led the Pay 'n Pak team to a third-straight national title, tying with the renowned Fort Wayne Zollner Pistons for the record of most consecutive titles. "Each of the championships that we won had a special meaning to the players," Wagner said, "but that one was on the top of the list of

Tom Wagner, one of the most successful fast-pitch softball managers.

achievements. After we lost that opening game (then won a record eleven games in a row) and I talked to the team, it seems like it was yesterday."

Wagner, sixty-five, compiled one of the outstanding records in fast-pitch, and had a winning percentage of .830, winning 917 games and losing 191. In ten ASA National Championships, his teams compiled a .810 winning percentage (47–10). His Pay 'n Pak and Peterbilt teams were some of the best in softball history, and Wagner wasn't one to play favorites on a team. "You are going to win with the best nine or ten guys. Sure, you have role players, but if you get to the national you aren't going to be changing your lineup every

special logo was designed by Galen Struve of Blue Springs, Missouri.

Other events that coincided with the Centennial included the Pan American Games in Indianapolis, Indiana, the U.S. Olympic Festival in Raleigh-Durham-Chapel Hill, North Carolina, and the Women's Friendship Series and the Men's International Slow-Pitch Cup, which was held inside the Hall of Fame Stadium and was the facility's first international event.

In 1986, for the first time in its history the ASA registered more than 200,000 teams. Andy Loechner of Pennsylvania was

re-elected president at the ASA National Council Meeting (November 11–17, 1986) in Honolulu, Hawaii.

The inaugural ISF Men's World Slow-Pitch Championship was held October 1–5, 1987, at the ASA Hall of Fame Stadium, with five countries participating. The Minneapolis Merchants, representing the United States, won top honors. There was even a slow-pitch exhibition game on October 3, matching Steele's Sports of Grafton, Ohio, against the Smythe Sox of Houston, Texas, with the latter winning 32–29. Thirty-nine homers were hit in the game. In the ASA Men's Major Fast-

Continued on page 86

Pay 'n Pak Ties Record

In 1987, Pay 'n Pak men's major fast-pitch team of Bellevue, Washington, concentrated on winning a record-tying third consecutive major fast-pitch title. That record had been previously established by Fort Wayne. Tom Wagner's Pay 'n Pak team took a shot at matching that record in the national championship held in Springfield, Missouri. Doing so seemed doubtful after their opening-game loss to Teleconnect of Cedar Rapids, Iowa with a score of 3–1. But Wagner's team annexed the title after running off eleven straight wins, including a victory over favored Penn Corp of Sioux City, Iowa, twice by 2–1 scores. "The first championship was special," Wagner said," but this one was equal to all of them."

In addition to being the third national in a row for the Bellevue-based team, the championship was the fifth title for them in the last eight years. They won two previous titles under the banner of Peterbilt Western with Wagner at the helm. Besides tying Fort Wayne's record of three consecutive national titles, Pay 'n Pak broke the record for most consecutive wins in the losers' bracket (eleven). Their pitcher, Graeme Robertson, equaled the record for most wins in a national championship (eight) including three on the tournament's final day.

But Pay 'n Pak might not have won the title if it weren't for the efforts of other players, whose clutch-time efforts helped clinch come-from-behind victories in three of the games. Jeff Borror did his part by hitting a grand slam to beat Guanella Brothers of Santa Rosa, California, 6–4, and Tourney MVP Bruce Beard pulled double duty by hitting a seventh-inning homer in the first game to force the if-necessary game and then driving in the winning run in the championship game. "If there's a key to our winning it's defense," said Wagner. "We try not to make defensive mistakes. We try to take advantage of the mistakes made by the opponents." That philosophy, combined with the players' talents and Wagner's leadership, paid off where it counts the most—in the won and lost column.

The 1987 Pay n' Pak team, after winning their third consecutive national major fast-pitch title.

Pitch National Championship in Springfield, Missouri, Pay 'n Pak of Seattle, Washington, came out of the losers' bracket to capture the title, equaling Fort Wayne's record of three consecutive national championships. Pay 'n Pak lost its opening game, then won eleven games in a row to annex the title.

The ASA Hall of Fame Stadium hosted the Tri-Nation Championship July 8–10, 1988, with the United States (represented by the Orange County Majestics of Orange County, California) sweeping five games (all shutouts) against Japan and China. Saskatchewan, Canada, hosted the ISF Men's World Fast-Pitch Championship in 1988. The U.S. Men's National Team defeated New Zealand

Top left: one of the dominant pitchers in the 1980s was Jimmy Moore, who starred for Pay 'n Pak of Seattle, WA Moore was elected to the ASA Hall of Fame in 2003. One of Moore's best seasons was 1985 when he was 54–5.
Bottom left: Ritch's Salvage of Harrisburg, NC captured the ASA Men's Major Slow-Pitch National Championship in 1989.
Right: although he didn't have a long career in fast-pitch, outfielder Brian Rothrock had some outstanding seasons playing in Decatur, IL (1981–1989) He was a five-time All-America and retired after the 1989 season.

4–0 in the championship game. It was the last time a U.S. team won this event.

The first seminar for commissioners was held February 23–25, 1989, at the ASA national office complex in Oklahoma City, with eighty-two commissioners attending. May 12–14 saw the first Advanced Umpires School, held in Oklahoma City. Sixty people, including five state-metro UICs and five ISF-certified umpires, attended the school. Also that year, the popular U.S. Olympic Festival—which was first held in Colorado Springs, Colorado, in 1978 with softball as one of the original sports—was held in Oklahoma City at the ASA Hall of Fame Stadium. The festival was part of a year-long state centennial celebration. It was in 1889 that the Land Run of Oklahoma took place, opening up the Oklahoma Territory for settlers.

For the first time, men's slow-pitch was part of the program as a demonstration sport, running July 22–25, with the men's and women's fast-pitch held July 24–28. A 3,000-mile torch run ran throughout the seventy-seven Oklahoma counties to conclude at the opening ceremonies, held in Norman, Oklahoma, inside Memorial Stadium on the campus of the University of Oklahoma. The

Remembering Rioux

· ·

When former Raybestos Brakette Allyson Rioux died of a brain tumor on February 9, 1989, her teammates didn't forget her. They dedicated the year to her, held a benefit game for her, and visited her grave in Connecticut. "We had a big benefit for her and most of us went up [to her grave] and talked to her before the game," former pitcher Kathy Arendsen said in the July 29, 1989, issue of the *Tulsa Tribune*.

"I just told her I missed her and she would always live in my heart. We dedicated this whole year to her." Arendsen, who pitched a one-hit shutout for the East in the U.S. Olympic Festival in Oklahoma City, said she felt Rioux's spirit throughout the festival. "I still can't believe she's gone," said Arendsen.

Unfortunately, Rioux is gone, but not from the memory and hearts of the Brakettes.

Second baseman Allyson Rioux helps up her opponent after being tagged out.

ASA Hall of Fame Stadium was recognized as the best venue of the thirty-seven sports during the event. Combining the two events (fast-pitch and slow-pitch) softball drew 13,998 people, with nearly 5,000 attending the slow-pitch competition.

For the first time, the Wilson/ASA Men's Super Slow-Pitch National Championship (held September 7–10 at the ASA Hall of Fame Stadium) was televised on ten regional sports cable networks. Twelve teams competed in the event, with the semis and finals shown as two two-hour segments.

CHAPTER VII

1990s

SOFTBALL CLEARS THE FINAL HURDLE

I n the early '90s, the ASA, other sports organizations, and businesses changed how they communicated with their customers and clients thanks to the birth of the World Wide Web. In the U.S. by 1994, three million people were online, and by 2007, 240 million people were online. Worldwide, 1.3 billion people were online. The ramifications of the World Wide Web were numerous, marking an informational revolution that continues to evolve today.

The World Wide Web helped the ASA more effectively communicate with and respond to the questions of its large membership thanks to e-mail, which has almost done away with hard-copy correspondence. In the process of updating its web presence, the ASA now owns six Web sites and a couple of Internet portals, making ASA information easy to find and user-friendly for fans and administrators alike. This information ranges from tourney fact sheets and current tournament results, to past champions, local ASA contact information and ASA National Hall of Fame members' stats, including pictures and bios.

Year after year, ASA online merchandise sales grow by leaps and bounds, and fans can purchase a wide range of ASA and USA Softball items, including replica Olympic jerseys of their favorite USA Softball player. The ASA now sells approximately eighty percent of its umpire uniform equipment online. The ASA Web site averages more than 200,000 visitors per month, accounting for over 1,000,000 page views per month.

While the ASA moved forward into this new era of communications, it didn't forget its responsibility to the people playing softball, and got women's slow-pitch in the 1990 Olympic Festival in Minneapolis. The top four finishing teams from the 1989 National Championship earned berths in the event, which a year earlier in OKC had featured men's teams.

The ASA realized getting softball into the Olympics would have far-reaching implications on the organization and the sport. This would mean not only fielding a team for 1996, but identifying and developing a

Continued on page 92

Facing page: this oversized softball from the Centennial Olympics in 1996 has signatures from all members of the gold medal-winning USA Olympic Team.

Softball and Olympic Status

Over the years, softball proponents learned to stifle their anticipation for getting their sport on the Olympic program. That was because no one knew when the sport would actually join the Olympic family and become a member of an exclusive athletic group. Year after year, as the IOC failed to grant softball the green light, the sport's advocates walked away feeling disappointed and frustrated, feelings ISF President Don Porter knows only too well.

Finally, on June 13, 1991, the IOC declared softball an Olympic sport. In the 1996 Olympics, softball made a memorable debut that left people speechless. The softball competition was played in Columbus, Georgia, at Golden Park, which was an appropriate name for the venue because the USA Team captured the first-ever gold medal for softball in a determined battle against China, 3–1.

The USA National Team repeated their gold medal-winning performance in the 2000 and 2004 Olympics, and won a silver medal in the 2008 Olympics in Beijing, China. But in July 2005, softball, as well as baseball, failed to hold majority interest and was voted out of the 2012 Games. The vote came as a shock to ISF President Porter, who had apparently misread the IOC's intentions after overhearing that

some IOC members were planning to vote for keeping the sport in the Olympics. "We thought we had it," Porter said. Jim Easton of Easton, one of the three USA IOC members, didn't vote because he felt he had a conflict of interest being a softball/baseball products manufacturer.

The ISF and others are awaiting the outcome of a critical IOC meeting in Copenhagen, Sweden, in October of 2009, when the committee will vote again to decide softball's Olympic fate. IOC President Jacques Rogge is determined to cap the number of Olympic sports at twenty-eight, the number of events at 300, and the number of athletes at 10,500. Rogge, according to IOC spokeswoman Emmanuelle Moreau, wants "to keep the size, cost, and complexity of the Games at a manageable level for organizing committees." If readmitted, the earliest softball could be expected is 2016, with Chicago, Madrid, Istanbul, and Tokyo vying to host the event.

ISF President Porter, who worked on softball's behalf as ISF secretary-general in the 1970s and 1980s, is lobbying again, traveling the world and hoping to restore softball to Olympic status. Under his direction, the ISF assembled a strategic task force and a "Back

IOC Director Gilbert Felli (left), ISF President Don E. Porter and ISF Secretary General Andy Loechner were on hand for softball's big announcement at the IOC annual session on June 13, 1991 that the sport would be in the 1996 Olympic Games.

Softball" campaign, which has a ten-issue agenda:

1. Increase the number of nations playing softball.
2. Increase the number of worldwide participants.
3. Increase the number of youth accessing sport through softball.
4. Place even greater emphasis on opportunities for women in sport.
5. Provide even greater worldwide access to people with disabilities.
6. Provide equipment/coaching where it is most needed.
7. Increase television coverage worldwide.
8. Increase the number of dedicated federations.
9. Improve the ISF administration so the best qualified people are in administrative positions.
10. Conduct the campaign in the true spirit of Olympism.

Part of the problem softball proponents face in getting softball back on the program lies in how the IOC members perceive softball. What softball is to an American IOC member is not necessarily softball to a European IOC member. "A lot of IOC members looked at us as women's baseball," Porter said in an interview with Brian Cazeneuve of SI.com ("Is Softball Too American?" February, 2008). "Some national federations combine softball with baseball, and we were lumped in with them. Prior to the vote in Singapore, the IOC released a sports evaluation report looking at how each sport fit the criteria for inclusion, and softball was right in the middle. I think a lot of IOC members never read the report." Baseball is facing a similar threat as an Olympic sport because the IOC isn't overly thrilled that major-leaguers won't be playing and that drug abuse is an ongoing issue within the sport.

Former Olympic swimming champion Donna de Varona and former IOC president Juan Antonio Samaranch are among the sports celebrities who have joined the "Back Softball" campaign. "To take this sport, when it's just taking root, and take away its Super Bowl is a death blow," de Varona said. "If the IOC is trying to make women's sports grow, the timing just doesn't make sense."

Lisa Fernandez, who has been a three-time member of the USA National team, also didn't mince any words on how she feels about the IOC's taking softball out of the Olympics—"It was devastating. I'm not even sure that's a strong enough word to describe how I felt. You think you're golden, you feel like you're at the top of the game, and all of a sudden it all gets taken away with no warning and really with no explanation." Fernandez and the rest of the USA Team, who toured the USA toting the slogan "Bound 4 Beijing," know 2008 could, for all practical purposes, be softball's last Olympics. The team's members are largely concerned that the next generation of soft-ballers won't know the feeling of taking the field in an Olympic softball event or wearing the red, white, and blue for the USA.

If the sport doesn't get back into the Olympics, then its players will revert back to playing in the ISF World Championships, the Pan American Games, the World Cup, and other regional events worldwide; but softball's best athletes may never again square off in worldwide competition as offered by the Olympics. Even if softball does get back on the Olympic program for 2016, players will have a seven-year wait before they can compete in the event, and it's a sure bet that softball will see a lot of changes, in funding and in personnel, in that time. Some of the people now involved in softball could be either retired or deceased by 2016, so new people will have to step up to help move softball into the future. Let's hope they get the opportunity to be softball's new Olympic torch-bearers. A bunch of ten- and eleven-year-olds are counting on them.

Above: two giants among the world of softball were W.W (Bill). Kethan (left), who was president of the ISF and Texas ASA commissioner, and Raymond Johnson, who served the longest as the ASA president and was the savior of the organization.
Facing page, top: Ralph Raymond of Worcester, MA, led USA to gold medals in 1996 and 2000 Olympic Games.
Facing page, bottom: this Netherlands fan certainly enjoyed cheering on his team during the inaugural Olympic softball competition.

generation of new players who would compete in the 2000 Olympics and beyond. To assist in getting softball into the Olympics, a player camp program was introduced in 1993 and expanded in 1994. To develop and maximize the talent of the best younger players in the United States, the ASA began the JO GOLD division in 1994 with the inaugural championship held at the Hall of Fame Stadium, August 10–14. Gordon's Panthers of LaPalma, California, won the first GOLD National.

The JO GOLD Championship was part of a 1994 television "triple play" that aired on ESPN2 on three successive weekends starting August 7. In addition to the JO GOLD, the other events of the triple play were the ISF Women's World Championship and the Women's Major Fast-Pitch National Championship. This coverage was made possible because, in 1993, the ASA helped

launch ESPN2 by televising the Men's Major Fast-Pitch National Championship from Decatur, Illinois.

Sadly, in a span of eight months, two people who had played major roles in the development of the ASA, Raymond Johnson and W.W. "Bill" Kethan, passed away. Johnson, third president of the ASA, died on August 10, 1991, at age eighty-seven, while Kethan died March 1, 1992, at his home in Jacksonville, Texas.

George Cron, who had helped Don E. Porter following Martin's death in 1962, passed away on April 19, 1994, from a heart attack while attending a board of directors meeting of the Golden Gloves Association of America at the Mark Plaza Hotel in Milwaukee, Wisconsin. Cron, eighty-two, served the ASA for fifty years and was one of six people in the Association's history to have reached that milestone.

Two years before his death, Cron, who served as chairman of the Joint Rules Committee on Softball from 1950 through 1975, was interviewed about the ASA and its growth. "Over the years with ASA, I have been fortunate to associate with some quality people," Cron said. "People in the field and people administering the sport from the national office. Quality people have made this organization into one of the top sports organizations in the world. The ASA has a great tradition of finding great people. And, once they get involved in the sport, they seem to stay with it over the long haul."

One of those people was Jack Aaron, executive director of the Texas ASA, who made ASA history as president during 1993 and 1994. He was the first ASA at-large player/rep ever elected to serve as the ASA's president, the association's highest non-paid position.

In July 1996, with the U.S. Olympic Festival held in St. Louis, Missouri, the ASA named Ralph Raymond of Worcester,

Massachusetts, as coach of its first Olympic softball team. "This is the pinnacle of my career. USA Softball is the best in the world and we are on our way to bringing home the gold in '96," Raymond said at the July 7th press conference announcing his selection.

Raymond, who managed the renowned Raybestos Brakettes of Stratford, Connecticut, to seventeen national titles, also led the United States to gold medals in the 1996 and 2000 Olympics. Assisting Raymond at the 2000 Olympic Games were assistants Shirley Topley of Anaheim, California, and Margo

Continued on page 97

DID YOU KNOW?

The Media

Before 1996, softball had to rely on getting its media coverage at selected events, including the U.S. Olympic Festivals, which attracted the top four placing teams from the ASA's Major Men's and Women's Fast-Pitch National Championships, the Pan American Games, the ISF World Championship, ASA National Championships, and various other events. When the media door swung open for the 1996 Olympics, softball appeared as one of the event's new sports, and the media response was overwhelming. Capacity crowds flocked to Golden Park, site of the Olympic softball competition, and the softball ticket became one of the hottest available for sale.

One ticket seeker positioned himself at the gates, attempting to trade his basketball "Dream Team" tickets even-up for softball tickets. "I've seen the 'Dream Team' and it was boring. I want to see what a real Olympic dream is all about," he said in the September 1996 edition of *World Softball*. Another fan called the media center and said he would pay $300.00 each for a pair of gold medal-game tickets. In addition to the fans who wanted tickets, the media wanted a seat for the gold medal showdown between the USA and China. The press seating for the gold medal game was about 110, but more than 160 media representatives were in attendance for the historic game.

Television unfortunately underestimated the sport's appeal as a national and international TV audience gleefully watched the recaps of the USA team, while fans made call after call to NBC wanting more. One study cited more than 4,000 U.S. – published articles about the sport's Olympic debut. Although a newcomer to the Olympics, softball's debut made its mark and clearly exemplified the ideals and spirit of the Olympics as fifteen young ladies gave a performance that was clearly awe-inspiring and one of the defining moments for both the 1996 Centennial Olympics and the sport of softball.

We at the ASA feel it was worth waiting all those years to finally get softball accepted on the Olympic program, and the 135,564 people who attended could attest to how the sport exemplified the Olympic spirit and caught the world's vision and respect.

The Decline of Men's Fast-Pitch

While women's fast-pitch, especially at the college level, is growing by leaps and bounds, men's fast-pitch in the United States is hanging on by a thread. The number of men's fast-pitch teams has dwindled from thousands to hundreds, and the number of teams participating in the ASA National Fast-Pitch Championship has fallen to fewer than twenty. The games are more high-scoring (9–6, 8–5) than in the old days. Back then, a score of one or two runs per team was typical, and an extra-inning game could throw the tourney's schedule off track. The fans would often attend an entire day's session, which could run from nine AM one day into the wee hours of the next.

Men's fast-pitch will never be what it was in the 1940s–1990s—the golden era—but it will continue to attract a dedicated bunch of players who love to play a game that demands razor-sharp reflexes, good hand-eye coordination, and tremendous skill. With the bases only sixty feet from home plate, fast-pitch forces players to "stay alive" and be alert at all times. If you're not this kind of player, the ball will whiz by you.

In today's fast-pitch world, the sponsors who have the money to operate and maintain a team (and who can fly players in) usually end up among the top finishing teams. Native-born American pitchers are a rarity at the men's major fast-pitch level, and the last American born pitcher to win an ASA major title was Chris Bigelow in 2000.

"In the 'good 'ol days,'" according to Ken Hackmeister, who has been involved in fast-pitch for decades, "there were far more teams, leagues, and tournaments than we have today. The sport was traditionally a small-town game where virtually every town had a league. If a town didn't have enough teams for a league, they simply had a town team. In some parts of the country, the local softball team or league attracted more fans than the counterpart minor league baseball team.

"Fast-pitch softball, which began as an outdoor game at the turn of the century, had its peak in popularity immediately following World War II. During the war, American servicemen introduced the game to other countries. At the war's end, the GI's returned home and continued playing fast-pitch softball in their local programs."

Hackmeister continues, "in the '50s, '60s and '70s, there were so many good teams that many never had to leave their state until championship tournament time, to play a full season of top-notch competition. Examples: California, British Columbia, Ontario, Iowa, Colorado, Minnesota, Texas and Aurora, Illinois. With fewer teams at the top level today [and few outstanding pitchers and a general overall lack of pitchers], the travel expenses take their toll. Some teams either fold their operation or drop down to a lower level of competition, where there are more teams to play against and thereby fewer travel expenses." In some cases, two teams may be combined.

"At the major or open level of men's fast-pitch there has been a tremendous sponsorship disparity among teams. In recent years, some sponsors are willing to spend upwards of $400,000 annually for their teams," says Hackmeister. "Contrast this with teams operating on a shoestring budget of less than $5000. Despite this disparity, teams at both extremes are operating at the same high level of competition. Another factor in this equation is that as time goes on there are fewer and fewer open- or major-class teams, most of them playing in the same invitational tournaments year after year. The travel expenses alone (air fare, motel rooms, car rentals, etc.) can be staggering.

"In an effort to save sponsor money, so that they can afford to pay travel expenses and to have international players, some teams opt to shorten their season to six weeks by not starting until late June or early

Left: one of the standout pitchers for the Fort Wayne Zollner Pistons, Clyde (Dizzy) Kirkendall compiled a 4–1 record with the Pistons in ASA National Championship play. He played from 1932–1953 and hurled 167 no-hitters.
Below: pitcher Dick Brubaker concentrates before hurling the ball.

July. What's worse is these teams still have to compete against opponents who not only have more money but have more practice and playing experience behind them. To offset this disparity many players of teams with low budgets will join other teams and play in a May or June Invitational."

Although fast-pitch isn't as strong as it was decades ago, there are signs of encouragement. Hackmeister notes that "various fast-pitch 'hot beds' continue to have numerous teams and local players." Stevens Point, Wisconsin hosted the ASA Men's Major Fast-Pitch National Championship for the first time this year and six of the seventeen teams were from Wisconsin.

Hackmeister also points out that "some late teenaged pitchers are coming out of the US Junior Men's National Team program and want to play at the highest level…[and] it would be encouraging to see younger developing players invited to US Men's National Team try-outs, so they get experience and a chance to mingle and play against the "big boys" for a few days."

He continues, "It would be more encouraging to see more big-money sponsors investing in young pitching prospects by taking them to all their tournaments, if for no other reason than to expose them to the game and let them see big-time fast-pitch at its best and what it is all about."

Unfortunately, some Parks & Rec tournaments have become "field rental organizations rather than being involved as tournament hosts and organizers." But we are living in tough economic times and parks and rec budgets are being reduced, too. Some Parks & Rec departments have also adopted a "no metal cleats" policy in their parks.

"And lastly," Hackmeister says, "it would be encouraging if more players, sponsors, administrators, and fans gave back to the game that has given them so much in terms of awards, entertainment, friends, and travel that they might never had experienced otherwise."

Nonetheless, men's major fast-pitch has had its share of outstanding players. Among them are Harold "Shifty" Gears, Ty Stofflet, Bill West, Harvey Sterkel, Herb Dudley, Bernie Kampschmidt, Bill Boyer, Clyde "Dizzy" Kirkendall, John "Cannonball" Baker, Tommy Castle, Hughie Johnston, Sam Lombardo, Roy Stephenson, Robert Forbes, Bill Wojie, LeRoy Hess, Weldon Haney, Bobby Spell, Frankie Williams, John Anquillare, John Spring, Bill Parker, Bonnie Jones, George Adam, Bob Barron, Eddie King, Abe Baker, Ron Weathersby, Doug Mason, John "Buster" Zeigler, Don Ropp, Vinnie Caserto, Elmer Rohrs, Leo Luken, Billy Stewart, Chuck D'Arcy, Glenn Beamon, Mike Parnow, Ray Phillips, Brian Rothrock, Harry Kraft, "Two-Gun" Joe Hunt, Butch Batt, Jimmy Moore, Dave Scott, Ronald Kronwitter, Warren "Fireball" Gerber, Jim Chambers, Noland Whitlock, David Grimes, Jerry Curtis, Ned "Ray" Wickersham, Joe Lynch, Metro Szyerk, Jim Brackin, Ted Hicks, Brian Rothrock, Ray Truluck, Tom Dallas, John "Sig" Lawson, Peter Turner, Ben Crain, Jim Ramage, Al Linde, Kermit Lynch, John Hunter, Roy Burlison, Avon Meacham, Peter Meredith, Dennis Place, Bobby Quinn, Stan Nelson, Harry "Coon" Rosen, Al Lewis, Sam "Sambo" Elliott, Clarence "Buck" Miller, Ricky Tomlinson, Bill Massey, Robert Kuykendall, Cannonball Bailey, Norbert "Cyclone" Warken, Michael White, Jody Hennigar, Brad Burrup, Marty Kernaghan, Cleo Goyette, Dick Brubaker, Mark Sorenson, Stan White, Shawn Rychcik, Leroy Zimmerman, Mike Piechnik, Tim Wahl, Darren Zack, Jack Randall, Darryl Day, Richie Stephen, Kevin Herlihy, Kenny Law, Chad Corcoran, Brian Martie, Les Haney, Todd Martin, Dude Ausmus, Paul Algar, Chris Delarwelle, Clint Herron, Ray Allena, K.G. Fincher, Doug Middleton, Lou Novikoff, Steve Schott, Brad Underwood, Ed "Fireball" Fiegelski, Bill Penick, Cam Ecclestone, Charlie "Choo Choo" Justice, Paul "Windmill" Watson, "King Kong" Kelly, Ernie Bertolini, Hoke Wilson, Dan Lipinski, Clyde Dexter, Mack Phillips, Ike Bierwagen, Eddie Tyson, Bunny Osborne, Dick Surhoff, Pat Campagna, Pat Marotta, Nazi Miller, Russ DeBerry, Clyde Wood, Julie Kujawa, Jeff Seip, Don Stainbrook, Roy Palmeri, Larry Silvas, Jay Bob Bickford, Brad Underwood, Don Sarno, Milt Stark, Ed Klecker, Randy Burnside, Sam Beavers, Clint Herron, Al Cotti, K.G. Fincher, Greg Sepulveda, Mark Smith, Nick Hopkins, Bob Todd, Paul Magan, and John Ege.

One of Ohio's top pitchers, Warren "Fireball" Gerber, won 608 games and lost only 93 during a 17-year career. He was 7–3 in ASA National Championship play.

Christa Williams

Christa Williams was a member of two USA Olympic Teams, 1996 and 2000. If it weren't for her dad, she might never have tried out. "I received a letter from USA Softball notifying me that my application to try out for the Olympic Team had been accepted. I was shocked and excited at the same time. I didn't even know I had applied," said Williams in the book, *Etched in Gold*. Ed Williams had sent in the application without telling his daughter, who at age sixteen became the youngest player to be invited to the 1994 USA Softball Women's National Team Camp.

The rest, as they say, is history. Williams was so impressive at the team camp that she earned a spot on the 1995 Pan Am Qualifier Team that won a gold medal in Guatemala.

Above: Christa Williams made the USA team in 1996 as a teenager. **Right:** Christa Williams hurling a pitch.

Williams went on to make the 1996 Olympic team and collected a pair of wins, fifteen strikeouts and a 0.00 ERA as the USA won the gold medal. She made the team again in 2000, winning a pair of games, hurling sixteen innings with twenty-three strikeouts and no earned runs. In two Olympics, she was 4–0 in 25.2 innings with thirty-eight strikeouts, eight hits allowed, no runs, no earned runs and only five walks.

Jonker of Mt. Pleasant, Michigan. Raymond's assistants in 1996 were Ralph Weekly (University of Tennessee) and Margie Wright (Fresno State).

The '96 Olympic softball competition was held at Golden Park in Columbus, Georgia (July 21–30). At the event, more than 8,700 fans witnessed the United States' victory over China in the gold medal game, 3–1.

"The year 1996 was a special time for our sport, especially women's fast-pitch," wrote Porter in the executive director's report. "The Olympics and softball finally got together and while it took long enough, it was worthwhile! The USA's gold medal victory did more to arouse the interest and spirit of millions of American than anything in the last twenty-four years in the sport of softball.

"While the competition lasted only nine days, it was a lifetime of work brought about by many people. Following the competition, our sport has been elevated to the status of a major international sport even though in most of our minds we were already a major international sport." The interest and publicity generated by the Olympics and especially the United States National Team had a profound effect on the ASA JO Program, which experienced more than a 13 percent increase from 1995 to 1999.

Throughout his career and into the nineties, Don E. Porter had worked tirelessly to get softball on the Olympic program. In fact, it was back in 1968 that he was first told by former IOC President Avery Brundage to have a lot of patience regarding getting softball into the Olympics. His efforts paid off on June 13, 1991, when it was announced that softball

would make the Olympic program in 1996 in Atlanta, Georgia. The announcement came from Birmingham, England, where Porter was joined by Loechner and O.W. "Bill" Smith of Nebraska. Porter had actually learned of the decision two days earlier when, standing near a balcony rail, he felt a hand on his shoulder. It was Juan Antonio Samaranch, IOC president. "He just smiled and said, 'Well, Mr. President, finally this is it,'" recalled Porter.

"It should be obvious that this is a major milestone for softball both in the USA and internationally. But what may not be as obvious is that it is also a major milestone for the Olympic program as a whole. Softball brings a vast audience of players and viewers to a program in critical need of more women participants. Softball has earned its day. We are happy that the International Olympic Committee agrees," Porter said in the

The Hall of Fame Olympic room has pictures and memorabilia of the USA's gold medals in the 1996, 2000 and 2004 Olympic Games.

Michele Granger

During her career, pitcher Michele Granger and her husband, John, lived in Anchorage, Alaska, after John took a job with an Alaskan Supreme Court justice. As one would imagine, such isolation could have presented a challenge for someone trying to practice. Not for Granger, now the mother of four children. "When you train for the Olympics in Alaska you have to be creative," Granger told the Standard-Speaker of Hazleton, Pennsylvania. Granger practiced by pitching in freight warehouses, into nets in her garage, and even in a church. "A protestant church allowed me to pitch in their basement," Granger said. "They didn't seem to mind that I was Catholic and that I was putting holes in their walls."

Granger hurled the opening and closing games of the 1996 Olympic Games when softball made its Olympic debut. She hurled 5 2/3 innings of the gold-medal game against China, with Lisa Fernandez finishing up in the circle. Where there's a will you can find a way—Granger certainly did.

Although she was pregnant, Michele Granger started the gold medal game of the Olympic Games in 1996. She's now the mother of four children and is a member of the ASA and ISF Halls of Fame.

sixtieth-anniversary commemorative issue of *Balls and Strikes* (August–September 1992).

On April 30, 1998, Porter, who had served thirty-five years as executive director, retired to devote his efforts to developing softball internationally and became president of the ISF. "It comes a time in everyone's life when one must move on and refocus their energies. Now is that time for me," Porter said. The ASA saw registration increases during thirty-three of Porter's thirty-five-year service. At the ASA National Council meeting in Nashville, Tennessee, he was recognized for his loyal and dedicated efforts when the Hall of Fame Stadium was re-named the Don E. Porter ASA Hall of Fame Stadium. Porter and former ASA National Office Executive Secretary Toma Malikoff were honored at the ASA Hall of Fame induction inside the Hall of Fame Stadium for their combined sixty-five years of service.

Porter, who earlier had by chance learned he had lymphoma and ultimately beat it, starting chemotherapy in 1989, had served the ISF as secretary-general and was elected president of the ISF in 1987.

DID YOU KNOW?

Men's Fast-Pitch Consecutive National Titles

Two men's major fast-pitch teams share the record for most consecutive national titles won with the same sponsor, the Fort Wayne Zollner Pistons (1945—1947) of Fort Wayne, Indiana, and Pay 'n Pak of Seattle, Washington (1985—1987). There is another men's team, however, that also won three consecutive Men's Major Fast-Pitch National Championships, but not with the same sponsor. The Clearwater, Florida, team came close by winning in 1950, 1957, and 1959, but these wins were not consecutive.

In 2000, the team, sponsored by Meierhoffer Funeral Home of St. Joseph, Missouri, went undefeated in the ASA Men's Major Fast-Pitch National in Nogales, Arizona. The team won its first ASA national title as Meierhoffer-Fleeman in 1998 and became only the fourth team in ASA history to go through a tourney and not allow any runs, outscoring the opposition 31–0 in thirty-three innings.

In 2001, the Meierhoffer-Fleeman team repeated as national champions, winning six of seven games in Decatur, Illinois—but this time it was under the name Frontier Players Casino. The team played as Frontier Players Casino in 2002 and stayed home to win the ASA national again, going undefeated and making that their third consecutive title and their second under one sponsor.

In 2003, the team hoped for a third consecutive national title under the Frontier Players Casino banner, which would have been their fifth overall, but they came up short in 2003, settling for a ninth place tie in Midland, Michigan. Apart from placing ninth in that tournament, the team also finished fifth in 1997 and 1999.

After that event, the team folded due to lack of sponsorship. A year later (March 13, 2004) the team's efforts were recognized with a special team induction into the Missouri ASA Hall of Fame.

Pennsylvania ASA Commissioner Loechner was elected as secretary-general to replace him. Loechner had previously served as ASA president (1986–1987).

Although Porter was the "point man" getting softball on the Olympic program, it must be mentioned that Porter's friendship with former IOC president Samaranch (who served l980–2001) certainly played a major role in his success. Samaranch attended softball's Olympic debut in Atlanta, Georgia, and his influence and power certainly can't be overlooked. Samaranch wanted to increase women's participation in the Olympics, and saw softball as an ideal sport to add to the program. The timing was right for both Porter and the sport. Now a recognized IOC honorary president for life, Samaranch on October 26, 2006, was named honorary chairman of the ISF task force (also known as "Back Softball"), a committee hoping that in 2009 the IOC will put softball on the Olympic program for 2016.

With Porter retiring from the ASA to serve as president of the ISF, a search committee, headed by former Tampa commissioner Jonathan Sinclair, was named to pick Porter's successor. Ron Radigonda, who did an outstanding job as the Sacramento, California, commissioner, was selected from a field of six candidates to succeed Porter in 1998. An astute businessman who knows the value of promotion and marketing, Radigonda moved the ASA forward at a time when adult softball participation had declined.

Unfortunately, Radigonda inherited a deficit budget of more than $1 million (accrued from 1992 to 1998), and the ASA was on the road to bankruptcy. The organization, for the first thirty-plus years of its existence, didn't have any competition, and as a result it hadn't felt the need to streamline its operations. Radigonda recognized the lack of foresight and worked to reorganize the national office and gradually improve the association's financial situation. Apart from the economic woes he faced on the job, Radigonda had to deal with health issues. Diagnosed with prostate cancer, he had surgery on April 8, 1998, but by June 1 he was at his office in Oklahoma City. He was impressed with the hundreds of supportive phone calls, letters, and cards he received.

In the past, the ASA had to borrow money to start the year. (Of course, in the warmer climates softball could for the most part be played year-round, but participation and revenue in the early months were minimal.) Since Radigonda's arrival, however, the ASA has had surplus budgets and made dramatic strides with its two additional fields at the Hall of Fame complex, better relations with Oklahoma City, expansion of the ASA gift shop, expanded television and marketing coverage of ASA events (including the World Cup of Softball, which has become one of the outstanding events of the sport), and modernization and expansion of the national office. Also thanks to his efforts, there is also now a master plan to add four more fields to the complex, which would give the association a total of eight championship fields suitable to host any of the outstanding JO National Championships.

With the growth of the events at the stadium, a facilities manager was hired. He schedules and plans the events at the stadium which, along with the television coverage, has helped expose and sell the ASA programs to today's new generation of athletes. The organization also moved forward in reorganizing its publications. On March 1, 1999, the ASA launched its first issue of *Balls and Strikes* on its Web site. The ASA also has used the Internet extensively and upgraded its Web site to market its programs and sell various merchandise and apparel.

Between 1995 and 1999, the ASA JO program increased more than 13 percent, from 73,756 teams in 1995 to 83,035 teams in 1999. The success of the 1996 USA National Team and the rise in college scholarship opportunities for girls' fast-pitch players probably played a part in the increases. In 1997, the ASA started registering individuals as well as teams, and the individual registrations reached 332,206 in 2007, with JO teams exceeding more than 86,000. Adult teams bottomed out at 125,347 in 2007.

On March 19, 2001, Charles L. McCord, former ASA president, Illinois commissioner and Hall of Fame chairman, passed away, after serving the ASA for fifty years. He was seventy-nine.

Having had successful Hall of Fame inductions in the past, the Hall of Fame Selection Committee, with the approval of the Board of Directors, elected to have the induction in conjunction with the ASA National Council Meeting. With the 2001 council meeting in North Carolina for the first time (in Winston-Salem), the Hall of Fame induction was a success, setting the tone for future inductions. Having the induction at the National Council Meeting after the season's end allows more people to attend. About 400 people attended the induction in Winston-Salem, and inductions since then have generated attendances between 400 and 620 people, proving the ceremony to be as popular with friends and family members as it is with the inductees.

In 2002, the National Softball Hall of Fame was renovated with trivia and highlights from the 2000 Olympics, making the exhibit more interactive. The lower level of the Hall of Fame also was renovated to include an historical timeline of the ASA, Junior Olympics, National Teams, umpires, the adult program, the Women's College World Series, and the Hooters USA Championship Series.

Also in 2002, the ASA did away with the points system for qualifying teams for the Gold Tournament, instead introducing Gold "sector" tournaments, with more tournament berths awarded based on registration numbers.

The U.S. Women's National Team staged one of the greatest comebacks in Olympic history, winning five consecutive games after three consecutive losses to take

Continued on page 106

Olympic Softball Recaps

1996

In the Centennial Olympic Games, with a record 197 nations competing, the USA National Team stepped front and center to bask in the media spotlight and capture the adulation of the thousands who attended the games and the millions more who watched on television.

And what an Olympics it was, as the USA answered the challenge of the other seven nations. The USA won its first four games easily, outscoring the opposition 29–1. They were then tested by a competitive Canada team, with the game tied at 2–all in the fifth before the USA tallied two more runs to win 4–2.

The USA's sixth game was as bizarre as you can imagine, though it was certainly entertaining, pitting two ace pitchers against one another: Lisa Fernandez of the USA versus Tanya Harding of Australia. Through nine innings, Fernandez was perfect, but the game could have ended two innings earlier if only USA's Dani Tyler had touched home plate after knocking one of Harding's servings into the seventh row of the center-field bleachers in the fifth. USA fans figured that was all Lisa needed to record the first perfect game in Olympic softball, but Tyler, who had a mental lapse after rounding third, simply passed by teammate Laura Berg, who stood in the on-deck circle, and never touched home plate. Australia noticed the mistake, appealed, and had Tyler called out for not stepping on home plate.

With the game continuing instead of ending, Fernandez and Harding battled with intensity and passion, knowing whoever made the next mistake could be the loser.

1996 USA Olympic Team. *Photo by Long Photography.*

2000 USA Olympic Team.

The USA scored a run in the tenth on a single by Sheila Cornell, with Dionna Harris, placed on second as per the international tie-breaker rule, scoring after Aussie center fielder Haylea Petrie threw wild to third base. Fernandez got the first two batters and, in facing Joanne Brown, was one strike away from getting the out she needed to end the game and be the first to pitch a perfect game in the Olympics. With an overflow crowd on the edge of their seats, Fernandez delivered what she hoped would be the third strike. Brown also delivered, sending the ball over center field for a home run and a 2–1 Australian win.

Despite that hard-breaking defeat, which denied Fernandez a place in the Olympic record book, the USA remained confident and beat China 3–2 and 1–0 in ten innings before facing them a third consecutive time with the gold medal hanging in the balance. The third time was the charm for the USA, who won 3–1 on a two-run homer by Dot Richardson in the third inning with Laura Berg on base.

The 1996 Olympic Games marshaled in a new era for the sport of softball. "It was like we stepped through a doorway from the past into the future," said USA pitcher Michele Smith. And the wait was worth it!

2000

With four years to train between events, it seemed there could be nothing but improvement from the other teams competing in the Olympics. And improvement there was, as the USA, despite a sometimes shaky defense, won its second gold medal thanks to an awesome pitching staff of Lisa Fernandez, Michele Smith, Lori Harrigan, Christa Williams and Danielle Henderson.

In ten games, the five fanned 132 batters, walked only fourteen, and allowed twenty-four hits. They allowed seven runs, only two of which were earned, for a team ERA of 0.15. The USA beat Canada 6–0 on Lori Harrigan's perfect game, and blanked Cuba 3–0 before losing to Japan 2–1, China 2–0, and Australia 2–1—the first time a USA National Team had lost three games in a row. The USA closed out the round-robin one game above .500 with a 4–3 record after beating New Zealand 2–0 and Italy 6–0.

In the medal round, the USA, not to be denied, disposed of China 3–0 and Australia 1–0 before defeating Japan 2–1 in the gold medal game. Lisa Fernandez hurled a three-hitter, fanned eight, and walked two in the circle for the USA. Making her second start in

2004 USA Olympic Team.

as many days, Fernandez trailed 1–0 on a Japanese homer by Reika Utsugi in the top of the fourth before the USA got even on an RBI single by Stacy Nuveman in the fifth. In the eighth, with pinch-runner Jennifer McFalls at second, Laura Berg hit a ball to deep left field. Japan outfielder Shiori Koseki played too shallow on the rain-slicked grass, came in and made a valiant effort but slipped and fell backward, dropping the ball from her glove. McFalls, meanwhile, crossed home plate with the winning run.

2004

With Athens as host, the 2004 Olympics will always be remembered as special for the USA National Team in more ways than one. First, the USA won its third consecutive Olympic gold medal, going undefeated in nine games with eight consecutive shutouts, including four run-rule wins. Second, the USA dominated the opposition, 51–1, and was anointed the "Real Dream Team" by *Sports Illustrated*, after the USA didn't allow a run until the sixth inning of its final game, beating Australia 5–1. And third, the USA

team had pursued the gold in the name of someone special, Sue Candrea, head coach Mike Candrea's wife, who passed away suddenly while on tour with the team in Wisconsin. Coach Candrea made the decision to go forward and lead his team because he knew that was what Sue would have wanted. To honor Sue during the Olympics, the team placed "SC" on the backs of their batting helmets and wore black wristbands with Sue's initials.

The USA blanked Australia in the first game of the Page playoffs, and met them again after the Aussies blanked Japan, 3–0 in the bronze medal game. Although it was the first time the Aussies reached the gold medal game of the Olympics, they would go home with a silver medal as the USA, behind Lisa Fernandez, won 5–1. The USA collected three home runs, including two, one in the first and one in the third, by Crystal Bustos. Her homer in the third inning was estimated at more than 300 feet and clearly was the longest homer hit in Olympic softball. And, besides going 4–0 in the circle, Fernandez batted a record .545 and was the competition's unofficial MVP.

Candrea's USA team was clearly the best women's softball team ever assembled and was perhaps the most dominant Olympic team of any sport. The USA team set eleven different Olympic records en route to the gold medal.

2008

The swan song of Olympic softball was a stunning upset. The USA Softball team lost to Japan 3-1 in the gold-medal game on August 21, 2008 in Beijing, China. The IOC voted softball out of the 2012 Games and the earliest it can return will be in 2016.

The loss denied the US a fourth straight gold medal and ended America's twenty-two-game Olympic winning streak. It was the first loss for US in Olympic competition since September 21, 2000 in Sydney, losing to Australia 2-1 in thirteen innings.

The US, which rolled through the round-robin, outscoring the opposition 53-1, advanced to the gold medal by beating Japan 4-1 in nine innings. Meanwhile Japan went twelve innings to outlast Australia, 4-3, to advance.

Japan's star pitcher, Yukiko Ueno, pitched all twenty-one innings, throwing 409 pitches and hurling another ninety pitches in limiting the high-powered US offense to only one run and five hits. One of those hits was an opposite field homer to right field by DP Crystl Bustos leading off the bottom of the fourth inning.

The other four USA hits were all singles, including two infield singles by Natasha Watley and Caitlin Lowe in the first. Lowe also singled in the sixth when the US loaded the bases and couldn't score. Pinch hitter Vicky Galindo singled in the seventh but the US couldn't muster a rally.

US starter Cat Osterman suffered her first loss in four games, hurling five innings, allowing two runs and three hits. Monica Abbott finished things up, hurling the last two innings, and allowing one run when Japan squeezed home the third run.

Osterman fanned five of the first six Japanese batters before Masumi Mishina doubled to left to open the third. Yukiyo Mine's sacrifice advanced her to third before Ayumi Karino's infield single scored her. Mishina's double was her first hit of the Olympics after an 0-for-21 drought. Japan scored their second run on Eri Yamada's HR to center leading off the fourth.

Japan, USA, and Australia softball teams spelled out "2016" using softballs following the medals ceremony in Beijing, hopeful that softball will be reinstated on the 2016 Olympic program.

home the gold medal in Sydney, Australia, in 2000. This performance brought softball, and especially the U.S. National Team, unprecedented worldwide media coverage, including the greatest amount of television coverage in the ASA's history. In addition to their appearance on the *Tonight Show*, the U.S. Olympic team players appeared on the NBC *Today Show* three times in 2000.

In 2004, the United States Olympic Team won a third gold medal in a dominating performance, allowing only one run in nine games led by the pitching and hitting of former UCLA standout Lisa Fernandez, who batted a record .545 and won four games inside the circle. "This team is the best I have ever been associated with," Candrea said of his Olympic team. "They are a 'special' group that will go down in history as the most dominant team to ever take the field. All of the countless hours spent in the weight room and on the practice field finally paid off for this exceptional group of athletes." The U.S. team broke no fewer than eighteen team or individual records.

Also in 2004, Mike Candrea, head coach at University of Arizona, was named to succeed Raymond as head coach of the United States, guiding the team to a third gold medal in Athens, Greece. He will also lead the United States at a chance for a fourth gold medal in China in 2008. After 2008, however, softball's Olympic status is in doubt. In fact, softball, which has been an unqualified success in the Olympics, didn't even get on the agenda to be considered for the 2012 Olympics. In 2009, the Olympic Committee will reconsider the inclusion of softball in the 2016 Games.

In 2006, the ASA Gold Championship, the premier event in the JO program, was held in Oklahoma City (August 6–13), and it returned in 2007 and 2008. The finals, broadcast on ESPN, attracted 200-plus college coaches to watch the premier girls'

players in America. The five acres the ASA selected for its Hall of Fame and national headquarters proved in the long run to be an ideal location (which, in later years was increased to twenty-five acres).

The ASA headquarters is located in a tourist area known as the Adventure District, which includes the following attractions: the renowned National Cowboy and Western Heritage Museum, certainly the crown jewel of the museums located in the Oklahoma City; the Oklahoma City Zoo; the Omniplex Science Museum; Oklahoma State Firefighters Museum; Cinemark Tinsel town USA Theatre; and Remington Park Racing Casino. The Adventure District has increased the visibility of all the attractions in northeast Oklahoma City, with the district attractions planning to invest $60 million in capital improvements by 2010. This is in addition to $39.6 million in capital expenditures made in 2005, the most recent year of complete records.

"To the Victor Go the Spoils"

Since 1996, for the teams that have played softball in the Amateur Softball Association, the saying, "to the victor go the spoils," has referred to the awards and trophies produced by MTM Recognition of Del City, Oklahoma. Dave Smith, the owner and founder of MTM, said, "Getting the ASA contract was a boost in building our business." The contract had previously belonged to Wilson Trophy, formerly of St. Louis, for twenty years.

Smith says, "The relationship was definitely a cornerstone in our foundation. ASA was a major sports organization with recognition on the national level. We appreciated the confidence placed in us and the association between MTM and ASA provided credibility to MTM in the sports arena. Our relationship with ASA was crucial in our development as a strong recognition company on a national level. We consider ASA a friend and a valued customer."

When Smith, a former basketball coach, started MTM more than thirty-five years ago, he had four clients. One of them was the Amateur Softball Association, which had moved to Oklahoma City in 1966 after spending fourteen years in Newark, New Jersey. As the ASA grew, so did MTM, which now occupies twenty acres and has more than 750 employees. "I'm most proud of our people," Dave said. "Our employees understand the value of recognition. We practice what we preach. They also see the fruits of their labor

in the media as well as local sporting and recognition events. The average tenure of our workforce is over fifteen years. Many people have been with me since the beginning. We have watched their families grow and have all made up the MTM family."

While the ASA has had its defining moments in its seventy-five-year history, MTM has had its share, too. One such moment occurred in 2001 when MTM acquired Josten's corporate recognition division. This acquisition allowed MTM to expand their market to include corporate service programs, safety and performance programs, and more. Of course, the acquisition also forced MTM to expand their infrastructure with regard to technology, manufacturing, and capacity. One thing about the recognition industry is that it is always changing and growing," says Smith. "Whether the economy is on the upswing or downturn, there is a need for recognition, on the ball field or in boardroom."

William Jones, a nineteenth-century philosopher and writer said, "The deepest principle in human nature is the craving to be appreciated."

Smith can relate. "As long as there is a need for appreciation, MTM will be there to meet that need through meaningful, symbolic awards of achievement. We are in the business of lifting spirits as our tag line states: Recognition Lifts the Human Spirit."

CHAPTER VIII

2000s

CHARTING A COURSE FOR THE FUTURE

Coming out of the 1990s, the ASA had made some progress and was on the road toward improvement. But there was still a lot to be done. The organization had reached a crossroads as people and organizations often do. Now at this crossroads, would it remain the ASA of old, which was slow and methodical to change and react, or would it move forward in a positive manner and make the changes in the best interests of the organization and its millions of members? The answer was uncertain.

What was certain was that the demographics of softball changed dramatically, with increased participation in girls' softball and decreased participation in adult softball, especially slow-pitch. The ASA seemed far removed from earlier days, when slow-pitch was its "bread and butter." Along with the declining participation came new softball organizations, all competing with the ASA for a piece of the ever-diminishing "softball pie."

Recognizing that the ASA needed to change how it did business, H. Franklin Taylor III of Richmond, Virginia, two-time ASA president (1978–79 and 2002–2003), along with members of the Oversight Committee and the Long-Range Planning Committee, initiated a long-range plan for the ASA.

In February 2002, the ASA hired a consultant (Steve Wolter of the Eppley Institute of Indiana University—Bloomington, Indiana) in order to gain a better understanding of the issues and concerns regarding the organization's outlook and its existing assets and liabilities. Since then, the ASA has kept on track with its long-range plan, which was developed through meetings and surveys of the ASA National Council, the Long-Range Planning Committee, and the ASA national office staff.

Realizing that this plan wouldn't succeed overnight, the Long-Range Planning Committee enacted a slow engaging process that

Facing page: sportsmanship was at its finest on April 26th, 2008 when Western Oregon senior Sara Tucholsky hit the first homer of her career. Doubling back to first base, her right knee gave out. Although she couldn't walk around the bases, she got a lift from Central WA's Liz Wallace (left) and Mallory Holtman. *Blake Wolf photo*

Sportsmanship
Mallory Holtman & Liz Wallace

When it comes to having character, Central Washington University softball players Mallory Holtman and Liz Wallace go to the head of the class. On April 26, 2008, Wallace and Holtman showed extraordinary sportsmanship and character when they helped injured Western Oregon senior Sara Tucholsky around the bases. The five-foot two-inch Tucholsky hit a three-run homer in the top of the second inning to give her team an early 3–0 lead. Tucholsky had only three hits in thirty-four at-bats this season prior to sending the ball over the center-field fence. Unfortunately, just hitting the ball over the fence did not seal the deal for Tucholsky, who missed first base on her homer. And when she turned back to touch it, her knee gave out (the injury was believed to be a torn anterior cruciate ligament).

At the time of Tucholsky's injury, the two runners who had been on base had already scored and were out of play and could not help her. Suddenly Sara found herself in the unpredictable situation of not being able to run the bases on the first homer of her collegiate career. And, given that Sara could not run the bases on her own, the umpires ruled that she could be replaced at first with a pinch-runner and have her hit recorded as a two-run single instead of a home run. They further ruled that if a coach or trainer assisted her around the bases, she would be called out.

Western Oregon head coach Pam Knox was ready to make a substitution when Holtman, a four-year starter for the opposing team, said, "Excuse me, would it be ok if we carried her around and she touched each bag?" The umpires agree that there would be nothing wrong with that, so Holtman and shortstop Wallace lifted Tucholsky off the ground and carried her around the bases, allowing her to touch each base.

"We all started to laugh at one point, I think when we touched the first base," Holtman told Graham Hays of ESPN.com." I don't know what it looked like to observers, but it was kind of funny because Liz and I were carrying her on both sides and we'd get to a base and gently, barely tap her left foot, and we'd all of a sudden start to get the giggles a little bit." The homer helped Western Oregon hold on for a 4–2 win but, as Holtman and Wallace showed, there is more to softball than winning and losing.

Since the game, the girls got more than their share of national media attention, including an appearance on *The Ellen DeGeneres Show* (May 7, 2008), and airtime on *Inside Edition*, the CBS *Early Show*, ESPN2's *First Take*, and ESPN's *SportsCenter*. CWU received hundreds of e-mails and phone calls from people touched by the story. Many sent donations to the CWU Foundation to support scholarships for future softball players. "We are definitely surprised by the response," said Holtman." I think it's exciting we've gotten so much great attention. It's good for softball and for Central."

allowed all ASA members to become familiar with the plan's need and purpose. This plan would guide the ASA into the future and address some of the issues and concerns, including identifying the priorities necessary to lead the organization with clear vision, and identifying how the commissioners, members, and staff could best react to current issues and anticipate future needs.

From 2002 to 2004, the Long-Range Planning Committee created a strategic road map for the ASA:

- Clarify the overall direction of ASA
- Foster effective decision making

- Anticipate and prepare the ASA for a preferred future
- Plan for the future based on ASA strengths and opportunities
- Promote accountability
- Anticipate customer and member needs

In short, the ASA, which has been a viable and high-producing organization for many years, wasn't reinventing or re-engineering itself, but was taking a look inward to define the challenges to its continued success. Such introspection was necessary for making the ASA an even better organization for the future. The ASA's legacy of service and commitment to softball is unparalleled, especially among nonprofit organizations.

The plan answered three questions: Are we doing the right things? Are we doing things right? And, what do we do next? To accomplish its goals, the Long-Range Planning Committee enacted a two-year process that involved and engaged all the ASA National Council members in the planning process. Ultimately, this long-range plan was adopted by the ASA's Board of Directors and offered the ASA a smooth transition into the twenty-first century.

Mick Renneisen of Bloomington, Indiana, served as chairman of the Long-Range

Planning Committee during this period and said, "Like all who have a passion for the sport of softball, I was concerned when participation in the sport began to decline. I was pleased that ASA leadership endorsed the idea of analyzing the reasons for the decline and also showed a willingness to take a look at the organization from top to bottom to

Continued on page 115

Below left: besides being an outstanding hitter and pitcher, three-time Olympian Lisa Fernandez could field her position well, either pitching or playing third base.
Below right: Lisa Fernandez was a member of three USA Olympic teams and was an alternate for 2008.

Softball in the 21ˢᵗ Century

While the twentieth century was marked by rapid development of travel fueled mostly by petroleum, the twenty-first century is marked by concern over how to cope with the consequences and resource depletion. For the ASA, the first year of the new century was one of both progress and sadness.

In 2001, the national council meeting was held for the first time in Winston-Salem, North Carolina, and it was the first year that the Hall of Fame induction was held during the meeting instead of earlier in the year. In previous years, since 1987, the ceremony had been held at the ASA Hall of Fame Stadium, and usually during the summer, when temperatures often soared above 100 degrees. Changing the time and venue was marked with overwhelming support, as more than 400 people showed up for the 2001 induction. Because that event was so successful, the annual induction is now always held during the national council meeting, drawing as many as 620 attendees.

On August 6, 2001, in an historic move, Pat Fleming of Iowa resigned as ASA president, citing that he had a new job and not enough time to devote to the ASA position. Past president G. Pat Adkison of Rainbow City, Alabama, assumed the role of president, until the council meeting in Winston-Salem. At that meeting, H. Franklin Taylor III of Richmond, Virginia, defeated E.T. Colvin of Columbus, Mississippi, by two votes to become president of the ASA for a second time. Ironically, Taylor had lost the election to Pat Fleming a year earlier.

Sadly, on February 26, 2001, Willie Klein, former managing editor of *Balls and Strikes*, the ASA's official publication, passed away at age eighty-seven. Then, on March 19, 2001, Illinois ASA commissioner, Hall of Fame chairman, and former ASA president, Charles L. McCord, passed away—a victim of stomach cancer. McCord had served the ASA for fifty years. He was

seventy-nine years old. "He was our leader and a tremendous advocate of softball," Don Brewer said. "He had a bunch of friends in Illinois and all over." Brewer later replaced McCord as Illinois ASA commissioner. And, to make matters more unbearable, a day after Charles's death, Hall-of-Famer Ruth Sears passed away at age eighty-three in Hemet, California. She was inducted into the ASA Hall of Fame in 1960 and starred for the Orange, California, Lionettes, earning four first-team All-America selections.

In 2002, ASA renovated the Olympic Room of the National Softball Hall of Fame to make it more interactive with trivia and highlights from the 2000 Olympics. They also renovated the lower level of the Hall of Fame, adding an historical timeline of the ASA, Junior Olympics, National Teams, umpires, the adult program, the NCAA Women's College World Series, and the Hooters USA Championship Series. In 2004, the United States Olympic Team, coached by Mike Candrea, won a third gold medal in a dominating performance, allowing only one run in nine games. Former UCLA standout Lisa Fernandez, through her pitching and hitting, batted a record .545 and led the team to win four games inside the circle. "This team is the best I have ever been associated with," Candrea said. "They are a 'special' group that will go down in history as the most dominant team to ever take the field. All of the countless hours spent in the weight room and on the practice field finally paid off for this exceptional group of athletes." The U.S. team broke no fewer than eighteen team and individual records.

In 2006, the ASA Gold Championship, the premier event in the JO program, took place in Oklahoma City (August 6–13) and returned in 2007 and 2008. The finals, broadcast on ESPN, attracted more than 200-plus college coaches to watch the premier girls' players in America.

2007 began with one of the ASA's best UIC workshops. About 400 people attended the biennial UIC Clinic, held February 9–10 at the Biltmore Hotel in Oklahoma City. Two people, Frankie Milan of Fort Worth, Texas, and Kinard Latham of Columbus, Georgia, were recognized for their fifty years of service to the ASA umpire program. Eighteen people received the ASA Award of Excellence. Mary Jane Cook, former national office employee, received the National Award of Excellence.

On a sad note, on the opening of the UIC clinic, famed barnstormer Eddie Feigner died at age eighty-one in the Cogburn Health and Rehabilitation Center in Huntsville, Alabama. Feigner had been touring with his four-man team since 1946. And on March 16, 2006, ASA Hall-of-Famer Herb Dudley passed away at age eighty-seven in Lynchburg General Hospital in Lynchburg, Virginia. Dudley's career spanned five decades, starting in 1940 and ending in 1981.

USA National Team pitcher Monica Abbott was named USA Collegiate Player of the Year for 2007. She pitched the Lady Vols to the championship game of the NCAA College World Series, which was the most-watched finale in history (1,676,000 households and a 1.8 rating). Later that year she was named the Sportswoman of the Year by the Women's Sports Foundation on October 15 in New York City.

The 2007 USA Men's Team finished runner-up in the ISF World Cup in Prague, Czech Republic, losing 2–0 to Japan in the gold medal game. The USA finished 8–3 overall. Long Haul of Durand, Wisconsin, proved it was best over the long haul by winning the ASA Men's Class A Slow-Pitch National Title on September 28–29 in Oklahoma City. They defeated defending champ Chaney's twice, 27–20 and 33–5, to conclude with a 5–1 record.

And, also in 2007, during the seventy-sixth national council meeting in Louisville, Kentucky, Andy Dooley of Bedford, Virginia, was named ASA president-elect. His opponent, G. Pat Adkison of Rainbow City, Alabama, was seeking a fifth term as ASA president. Dooley will officially take office at the 2009 council meeting in Reno, Nevada.

In 2008, Laura Berg, former Fresno State star, closed out her career as the only four-time Olympian in the history of softball by being named to the fifteen-member U.S. National Team.

2008 also marks the ASA's recent announcement that it has plans for a new $550,000 scoreboard, and that the people of Oklahoma City have voted for a $4-million bond for ASA Hall of Fame improvements, including a new press box and a locker room-umpire-meeting room. The renovations are scheduled to start sometime in 2010. Future plans include expansion of the ASA National Softball Hall of Fame, possibly in 2014.

Carol Spanks

What did the ASA mean to Carol Spanks, a member of the ASA National Softball Hall of Fame and one of the greatest players in women's fast-pitch? Spanks played for twenty-three years.

"Mainly, it meant having a place to play that included special tournaments for the better players such as regionals, nationals and all-star games. Having played under the auspices of the ASA from the mid-1950s through the mid-1970s this was about the only way to experience top-quality competition. I have enjoyed some opportunities through softball as a player and coach internationally as well."

Spanks, who was an outstanding college coach as well (Cal Poly Pomona and University of Nevada-Las Vegas) also listed some defining moments in her outstanding career. They included:

- As a player being a member of a world championship team (Orange Lionettes) in 1962.
- As a player/coach, qualifying for the Second ISF World Championships as the USA representative in 1970.

As coach, being involved with the 1987 Pan American team: "From tryouts in Colorado Springs when there was an awesome selection committee through all the practice games and winning the gold medal with a staff that was terrific right down through the members of that undefeated team. The friendships made and the experiences we had will never be forgotten."

Softball Attitude

Explaining how Carol Spanks played fast-pitch during her twenty-three-year career would be like explaining someone's desire to drive a car fast. Each would have the throttle all the way out.

The most difficult thing for Spanks to do was to retire from playing. And that was after a season in the professional women's league (1976), following a Hall of Fame career with the Buena Park Kittens, Buena Park Lynx, and the Orange, California, Lionettes, which came out of the Lions Club of Orange, California. After retiring as a player, Spanks turned to coaching, first at Cal Poly Pomona (1978–1993), then at the University of Nevada, Las Vegas, (1995–1999).

During her stay at UNLV, Carol noticed a change of attitude in women's fast-pitch. "It was there that we had 'full' rides and many products given to us by sponsors. You began to get evidence of more change while in the recruiting process," Spanks said.

"It seemed, at the beginning of scholarships, players (and parents) were more concerned, for the most part, in what their daughter would get financially than they were in the quality of the school, coaching, program in general, etc.

"Then, with the advent of Olympics, and opening the door to the players getting sponsors, paid for services, etc., it really went out the door." Spanks isn't saying these changes were good or bad. "I am not making a judgment one way or another as to the best of ours and current players' attitudes, but there definitely is a difference."

A star athlete at Pasadena City College, Spanks played in a different era, and the philosophy of the players then was entirely different from that of players now. "Most of us [players in her era] got nothing for playing amateur ball. (Of course some teams with sponsors got money under the table), but I personally never experienced that. Whatever was provided for the team each person got the equivalent…such as gloves, shoes, etc. We thought it pretty great that it didn't actually cost us to play ball.

"Although the game has changed drastically, and women are now able to make a living at playing ball, I envy them at times. It was always a big 'what if' for those of us who loved to play ball could have made a living doing it, such as baseball players.

"On the other hand, I wouldn't trade the excitement and opportunities we had while playing. The structure lent itself to some pretty stable teams competing annually for the big prize [the ASA National Championship]. The competition was fierce; the crowds great and the seasons were filled with many special events (ASA All-Star Series) and things to look forward to. I can recall hearing Don Porter speak annually about how close we were to becoming an Olympic sport. This was in the '60s and '70s."

Finally, after so many false alarms, softball became an Olympic sport in 1991. Spanks was still coaching then, but her memories are priceless, and she is one of a number of outstanding players left wondering, What if softball had become an Olympic sport much earlier?

Although shortstop was her normal position, Carol Spanks could pitch for her team from time-to-time during an outstanding 23-year career.

see if there were ways to improve an already outstanding organization.

"I've been honored and consider it a great responsibility that four different ASA presidents have allowed me to lead the initiative as the Long-Range Planning Committee chairperson. Even more importantly, it has been extremely gratifying to see that recommendations from the Long-Range Planning Committee have been accepted and adopted by the ASA Board of Directors and ASA National Council and these recommendations may lead to improving our great organization and lead to enhanced opportunities for those who participate in the many different options (programs) governed by ASA."

The ASA long-range plan is a work in progress, according to former ASA President E. T. Colvin, who played a major role in

changing the mindset of the Association and pushing forward a philosophy of accountability, which had been ignored for many, many years. "We are in the fifth year and about to start the second phase," Colvin said. "[The Long-Range Plan] is something that the ASA should have had in place many years ago. The main issues we are addressing are accountability of the local associations, developing a way to grade the progress or lack of success or productivity of the local association. We are addressing the restructuring of the ASA and the geographic boundaries of the ASA.

"A report card has been developed to evaluate each local association and a fourth of the local associations were evaluated in 2006 and the same amount will be evaluated each year until all have been done. The restructuring was further investigated in 2007. And legislation will be proposed to make some

Eddie Feigner
Last of the Great Barnstormers

• •

When Eddie Feigner (pronounced FAY-ner) died on February 9, 2007, it marked the passing of the last of the great barnstormers. Feigner was eighty-one. Since starting the King and His Court in 1946 on a dare, Feigner and his four-man team toured throughout the USA and the world, traveling 4,100,000 miles and entertaining more than twenty million people. In 1998, the Court became a three-man, one-woman team with the addition of Eddie's wife, Anne Marie Feigner. Anne Marie, who managed to keep the Court going following Eddie's passing, eventually turned it over to the North American Booster Club Association and its executive director, Steve Beden.

Eddie Feigner would pitch blind-folded—from second base—and delight fans with his antics and pitching show at the end of the game. But after sixty years on the road, Eddie passed away just about broke and needing donations gathered through his Web site to continue to live and pay for mounting medical bills. No one knows how much money Feigner went through. The best guess would be in the millions, and softball pitching was the only way he could survive in this world, and because of that he kept hitting the road year after year. His health finally caught up with him. In the end, Feigner enjoyed what he did for six decades, entertaining and making a living pitching a softball. He was one of a kind, and there probably won't be another one of his equal.

With the exception of the Court, which continues to tour, today there are no other touring teams. There probably won't be any more, either, as society today is much different from that of 1946, and things are more expensive now. And, although the King and His Court have been around the longest, during their existence there have been a number of barnstorming teams, including the Silver Sixes, featuring ASA

Eddie Feigner of the King and His Court barnstorming team thrilled millions of fans for 60 years before passing away in 2007 at age 81.

Hall-of-Famer Metro Szeryk; the Oklahoma Cowboys; Hop and the Hustlers; Jack and the Jesters, featuring Rusty Jack Sparks; 4's Enough; Ace Holden and the 4 Rockets; the Prince and the Knights; the California Cuties; the Iowa Ghosts; the Colored Ghosts; the Philadelphia Hoboes; Softball Fever; and the Queen and Her Maids, which started in 1962 and lasted through 1990. They later were called the Queen and Her Court because Eddie taught Rosie Baird Black how to pitch.

changes. This process is necessary to ensure the success of the ASA for the future."

Change is inevitable. Change is also uncomfortable. Change is good. Change is great. Some say, "You go first," and others say, "Change is good as long as it doesn't affect me." Fortunately, the ASA is now making the changes necessary to move the organization forward and operate in a more professional, business-like manner.

As the ASA reflects on its seventy-five years, it can point with pride to the many people and volunteers who committed their time and efforts to moving the organization forward. These people have given untold hours and effort in the best interest of the ASA. The early organization years were not without resistance. Many of the promoters and profiteers of the sport found it difficult to turn over the reigns of leadership. There were more, however, who loved the sport and wanted to see it flourish over any plans for their own personal gain. The people who have been involved with the ASA are proud of the organization and its accomplishments, which are legendary, and proud they should be because there is only one national governing body of softball, and it's the ASA. Sure, it wasn't easy; but if it were easy, it wouldn't be worth pursuing.

Since its founding, the ASA has given millions of adults and children the opportunity to play a lifetime sport and experience its thrill, whether in a national championship, an Olympic Festival, the Pan American Games, the Olympic Games, or in a city recreation league a couple of times a week.

Softball has been the sport of the masses, and the ASA has been the organization to move it forward, sometimes against overwhelming odds, to do what is in the best interest of the sport. Because of the tremendous job the ASA has done, softball is better for it, and the millions of people who have played ASA softball are better for it—thanks

Eddie Feigner, star hurler for the King and His Court, won more than 8,700 games during his legendary 60-year career.

Unrealistic Expectations

People who have played softball—or any amateur sport for that matter—have long been passionate about their pastime and the joy of competing. There is nothing wrong with being passionate. In recent years, however, some parents, fans—and in some cases, coaches—appear to have developed an unhealthy perspective about the sport. They seem to have forgotten that to participate in a game is to take part in an education about life. Instead, they view their participation as being part of a "life or death" struggle for dominance. Values such as sportsmanship, self-esteem, getting along with others, integrity, and honesty are thrown aside for "winning at all costs." Perhaps Dr. Steve Clarfield, author of *Softball's Lefty Legend: Ty Stofflet*, is right: "Nearly every day we get assaulted by some reminder that sports and sportsmanship are not connected. Whether it's at the local, state, national or international level, there seems to be a constant stream of events that don't get past the 'smell test' for being right."

Furthermore, some people appear to have lost keen perspective on what they feel they should get from a particular sport. For example, consider parents who spend thousands—on camps, clinics, lessons—for their daughter to participate in softball. Such devotion on the part of the parents is commendable so far as the intent is to offer their child what they feel is the best experience possible. However, the devotion can become condemnable when the parents demand a return on their investment by expecting that their daughter be chosen to play at increasingly higher levels. Expecting such a return is unrealistic given that in the reality of sport there must be losers as well as winners, and ascending to a higher level requires that only a limited few move on.

Not everyone is going to make the U.S. Olympic Softball Team (only fifteen players make the cut), and not everyone is going to start as a freshman at Arizona or one of the top softball schools and universities. A precious few make the jump and go on to succeed at the Division One level or whatever college level of softball they play. And the pro softball players know they are wise to keep their day job. The majority of athletes who play college softball should feel fortunate that they got a scholarship for something they love to do—play softball. The majority, however, never achieve the dreams their parents laid out for them from the day they started playing T-ball—and these are the people who take up recreational softball and play a few times a week. But that is the beauty of softball. It's a lifetime sport and the millions of seniors who play can attest to that by the hundreds of games some play each season.

It's time that we all take the time to center our perspective and recognize that true champions have respect for themselves, their teammates, opponents and the game itself.

to Pauley and Fischer, who decided it would be a good idea to start a sports organization in the worst of times.

The main entrance to the ASA National Softball Hall of Fame in Oklahoma City, which has more than 120,000 visitors each year.

APPENDIX A
ASA PRESIDENTS

Throughout its seventy-five-year year history, the ASA has had thirty-five different people serve as president, the highest non-paid position in the organization. Some served one year, some two years—one president even served four times (G. Pat Adkison of Rainbow City, Alabama). The common thread tying these people together is their involvement in softball, although some of their "real" job titles include lawyer, YMCA director, insurance salesman, recreation director, business owner, and sports editor.

The duties of the president include, but are not limited to: presiding at all sessions of the Board of Directors and National Council; appointing all committees; creating ad hoc committees; serving as an ex

officio member of all committees; coordinating and approving the agenda for all meetings of the BOD with the executive director; delegating duties and authority to the executive director; determining the site of BOD meetings; and coordinating a mail, fax, or telephonic vote from the BOD for any expenditure that will exceed a budgetary line item.

Three presidents served the ASA at least fifty years: Fred Hoffman, Charles L. McCord, and Joseph Barber. All are deceased.

Without these people and the others who helped and supported them, the ASA wouldn't be celebrating its diamond jubilee. A debt of gratitude and thanks goes to all of these people for the leadership they've provided for the past seventy-five years.

Leo Fischer, 1933–39 (deceased)
Fischer and M.J. Pauley co-founded the ASA in 1933.

Wilbur E. (Bill) Landis, 1940–42 (deceased)
Landis was one of the pioneers of the ASA. He played a major role in the development of softball and other sports for Briggs Beautyware Company, Detroit, MI.

Raymond Johnson, 1942–48 (deceased)
Regarded by many as the savior of the ASA, Johnson
was the longest-serving president of the organization.

Nick Barack, 1949–50 (deceased)
Along with Bill Kethan, Barack was instrumental in
the formation of the International Softball Federation.

Walter Hakanson, 1948 (deceased)
Hakanson is credited with giving softball its name.

James Lang, 1951–52 (deceased)
Lang was the first person from San Francisco to
become ASA president.

Louis Canarelli, 1953–54 (deceased)
Canarelli was the former Supervisor of Education, Newark, NJ Board of Education. He was a graduate of Panzer College and held a master's degree from NYU.

Otto Smith, 1957 (deceased)
Smith managed a post office team in Little Rock, AR, and led them to victory at the first Arkansas state championship in 1932.

John Deaver, 1955–56 (deceased)
Deaver helped to organize the first ASA Men's Slow-Pitch Championship in Cincinnati in 1953.

Ford Hoffman, 1958–59 (deceased)
Hoffman had a varied background as a player, coach, manager, commissioner, and area vice president.

Fred Crosby, 1960 (deceased)
Crosby served as Maryland ASA commissioner from 1937 to 1965.

Fred Hoffman, 1962–63 (deceased)
Hoffman served the ASA for fifty years and was Missouri ASA commissioner.

George Cron, 1961 (deceased)
Cron served the ASA for over fifty years, and was also the chairman of the IJRCS from 1950 to 1975.

W.W. (Bill) Kethan, 1964–65 (deceased)
Kethan was a pioneer of softball both in the USA and internationally. He served as president of the International Softball Federation from 1965 to 1986.

Ralph Guynes, 1966–67 (deceased)
Guynes was the first person from Northwest to serve
as president.

John Nagy, 1970–71 (deceased)
John Nagy was Cleveland ASA Commissioner and
was a 1937 graduate of Ohio State University.

Fred Blum, 1968–69 (deceased)
Blum was a graduate of the Cornell Law School
and was the Rochester ASA commissioner for
twenty-five years.

Eddie Moore, 1972–73 (deceased)
Moore managed the Clearwater, FL, Bombers to four
national titles and four runners-up in twelve years.

Joe Barber, 1974–75 (deceased)
Barber has served as ISF vice president and Hall of Fame Selection Committee chairman. He is a member of both the ASA and ISF Halls of Fame.

H. Franklin Taylor III, 1978–79 and 2002–03
Taylor has the distinction of serving as president twice, in addition to being Central Virginia ASA commissioner for thirty-five years.

Andrew Pendergast, 1976–77 (deceased)
Pendergast was Washington ASA commissioner from 1954–1986. He was a native of Syracuse, NY, where he worked for the recreation department.

Howard Honaker, 1980–81
Honaker served as Ohio ASA commissioner from 1969–2006. He had a forty-seven-year career with Faultless Rubber Company.

Arnold (Red) Halpern, 1982–83 (deceased)
Halpern served as Idaho ASA commissioner from
1958–2003. He was the Parks and Rec director in
Coeur d' Alene, ID.

Andrew S. Loechner, 1986–87
Loechner was named Pennsylvania ASA commissioner in 1972. He has been the secretary-general of
the International Softball Federation since 1987.

Charles L. McCord, 1984–85 (deceased)
McCord served the ASA for fifty years. He was chairman of the National Softball Hall of Fame Committee
from 1958–90, and Illinois ASA commissioner.

Bert Weeks, 1988–89
Weeks served as the North Carolina ASA commissioner from 1974–2005 and was the softball venue
manager at the 1996 Olympic Games.

O.W. (Bill) Smith, 1990–91
Smith was ASA president when the news came that softball had been accepted as an official Olympic sport in 1991.

Jack Aaron, 1993–94
Aaron is the first at-large player-rep ever elected president. He is former Texas ASA commissioner and is now executive director of the Texas ASA.

G. Pat Adkison, 1992, 1999–2000, 2001
Adkison is the only four-term president in ASA history. He was elected three times, and took over when Pat Fleming resigned in 2001.

Wayne Myers, 1995–96
Myers has served as the ASA Indiana commissioner since 1976 and was ASA vice president before becoming president. He is also a former fast-pitch pitcher.

Bill Humphrey, 1997–98
Humphrey was instrumental in starting the ASA
National Umpire Schools with Ron Jeffers and Tom
Mason.

E.T. Colvin, 2004–05
Colvin is the Mississippi ASA commissioner and a
member of the Long-Range Planning Committee.

Pat Fleming, 2001
Because of work commitments, Fleming was unable
to complete his term as president.

D. Stephen Monson, 2006–07
Monson is the former Southern California ASA
commissioner.

Joey Rich, 2008–09
Rich is the second person from Missouri to serve as ASA president.

Andy Dooley, 2010–11
President-elect Dooley will take office following the 2009 National Council meeting in Reno, becoming the thirty-sixth person to hold the position.

APPENDIX B
HALL OF FAME
MEMBERS

Commissioners

1976: Nick Barack
1976: W.W. (Bill) Kethan
1976: Fred Hoffman
1976: Einar Nelson
1976: Carl Kelley
1977: John Nagy
1977: Benny Turcan
1977: Lou Hamilton
1978: Ed Clott
1978: Joe Barber
1978: Jerry Stremel
1979: Andrew Pendergast
1979: Al Bishop
1980: W.B. (Bick) Auxier
1980: Matt Urban
1980: George Cron
1981: Arnold (Red) Halpern
1982: Don Sndyer
1982: Fred Crosby
1982: Fred Blum
1983: Duane (Tiny) Schafer
1984: Lewis Brasell
1985: Jack Spore
1986: O.W. (Bill) Smith
1987: Alfred (Red) Morton
1988: Howard Honaker
1988: John Deaver
1989: Andrew S. Loechner
1990: Bert Weeks
1991: H.Franklin Taylor III

1993: Elliott Hawke
1995: Fran Mott
1999: G. Pat Adkison
2000: Wayne Myers
2003: Cliff Warrick
2004: A.C. Williams
2004: Ed Lindsey
2006: Pat Lillian
2008: Garland Thompson

Umpires

1976: George Dickstein
1976: Bernard Iassogna
1976: Art Solz
1976: Robert (Dirty) Deal
1977: Ron Derr
1979: Ferris Reid
1980: Ivie Apple
1980: Harold Adams
1980: Frank Susor
1982: Tom Mason
1992: Eddie Mayhew
1983: Bob Quillen
1983: Ed Dressler
1987: Bill Humphrey
1987: Henry Flowers
1988: Rex Brown
1989: Bill Finley
1991: Merle Butler
1992: Henry Pollard
1992: L. R. (Tarz) Timm

1993: Dan Blair
1993: Billy Monk
1993: Bernie Profato
1999: Herman Beagles
2000: Billy Peterson
2001: Walter Sparks
2001: Horace Bruff
2002: Jerry Hanson
2004: Emily Alexander
2005: Nick Cinquanto
2005: Craig Cress
2006: Ralph Miller
2007: Dave Epperson
2008: Kevin Ryan
2008: Ron Galemore

Meritorious Service

1976: Raymond Johnson
1976: Leo Fischer
1977: Charles L. McCord
1977: Bob Hoffman
1977: Charles Jensen
1979: Bernard (Bunny) Lee
1980: James F. Jones
1980: Nick Frannicola
1980: Harold Engelhardt
1981: Charles (Budd) Gilbert
1981: Arthur Noren
1981: Vince Scamardella
1982: Percy Hedgecock
1982: Eddie Moore

1983 Margaret Nusse

1983 Cliff Smith

1986 Mack Phillips

1988 Don E. Porter

1989 Tom E. Beck

1990 Bill Svochak

1991 Kay Purves

1993 Jim Carman

1994 Dick Reinmiller

1994 Buck Johnson

1995 Jack Aaron

1996 Lewis Rober Sr.

1998 Claud (Chuck) Davenport

1999 Bill Plummer III

2001 Kinard Latham

2002 Marty McGuire

2004 Bill Williams

2005 Bob Savoie

2006 Don Brewer

2006 Norm Davis

2007 Jack Mowatt

2008 Jerry Stewart

2008 Freddie and Virginia Ezell

Managers

1976 Commie Currens

1976 Willard Fenton

1977 Vincent Devitt

1977 George (Doc) Linnehan

1977 Bud Gagel

1978 LeRoy Rutenschroer

1978 Duke Denson

1979 Johnny Moon

1980 Marge Ricker

1980 Ford Hoffman

1983 Bobby Lutz

1984 Al Brausch

1984 Bill Caye

1985 Erv Lind

1988 Maxine Thayer

1988 Roy Lombardo

1988 William (Red) Jenkins

1989 Charles Keeble

1993 Ralph Raymond

1993 Rocky Santilli

1998 Dave Neale Sr.

2000 Russ Boice

2002 Tom Wagner

2003 Eugene Kwalek

2007 Hank Bassett

Sponsors

1976 William Simpson

1976 Fred Zollner

1976 Charles Hurd

1976 William Pharr

1982 Richard Howard

1992 Fred and Karl Nothdurft

1992 Jerry Pendergast

1993 Harry (Robbie) Robinson

1994 Woody & Pat Bell

1997 Abbott Labratories

1998 Walt and Ray Guanella

1999 Immor Clyte Franklin

2002 Bill Fraley

PLAYERS

Men's Fast-Pitch

1957 Harold (Shifty) Gears

1957 Sam (Sambo) Elliott

1958 Al Linde

1959 Bernie Kampschmidt

1959 Clyde (Dizzy) Kirkendall

1960 Warren (Fireball) Gerber

1960 Clarence (Buck) Miller

1960 Jim Ramage

1961 John (Cannonball) Baker

1961 Ben Crain

1961 Hughie Johnston

1963 John Hunter

1963 B. E. Martin (non player)

1963 Bill West

1964 Tommy Castle

1965 Roy Stephenson

1966 Jim Chambers

1966 Robert Forbes

1967 Noland Whitlock

1967 Bill Wojie

1967 Ronald Kronewitter

1968 LeRoy Hess

1968 Bob Sprentall

1970 John Spring

1970 Frankie Williams

1971 John (Buster) Zeigler

1971 Ned (Ray) Wickersham

1972 Don Ropp

1972 Jerry Curtis

1973 Richard Tomlinson

1974 Charles Justice

1976 Bobby Spell

1978 Tommy Moore

1978 Doug Mason

1979 Bill Massey

1979 Weldon Haney

1980 Ron Weathersby

1981 Harvey Sterkel

1981 Bill Parker

1981 George Adam

1983 Bonnie Jones

1983 Robert Kuykendall

1984 Bob Barron

1986 Herb Dudley

1988 John Anquillare
1988 Vinnie Caserto
1988 Al Lewis
1989 Joe Lynch
1989 Carl Walker
1990 Harry (Coon) Rosen
1990 Abe Baker
1991 Eddie King
1991 Sam Lombardo
1992 Elmer Rohrs
1993 Leonard (Leo) Luken
1996 Ray Allena
1996 Stan Nelson
1996 Billy Stewart
1996 Jim Brackin
1996 Ray Truluck
1997 Roy Burlison
1997 Chuck D'Arcy
1998 Mike Parnow
1998 Tom Dallas
1999 Glenn Beamon
1999 Ray Phillips
2000 Brian Rothrock
2000 Denny Place
2000 Ted Hicks
2001 Bobby Quinn
2001 Harry Kraft
2002 Butch Batt
2002 John (Sig) Lawson
2003 Bill Boyer
2003 Jimmy Moore
2004 Jeff Borror
2004 Metro Szeryk
2004 Ty Stofflet
2005 Dave Scott
2006 Avon Meacham
2007 Peter Turner
2007 Dave Grimes
2008 Jim Marsh
2008 Kermit Lynch
2008 Mitch Munthe

Men's Slow-Pitch
1973 Myron Reinhart
1974 Frank DeLuca
1975 Don Rardin
1982 Bill Cole
1984 J.D. McDonald
1985 James Galloway
1986 Hal Wiggins
1987 Carl (Tex) Collins
1988 Eugene Fisher
1989 Raymond Brown
1989 Mike Gouin
1989 Eddie Zolna
1990 Dick Bartel
1990 Tom Beall
1990 Ken Clark
1992 Lou Del Mastro
1992 Paul Tomasovich
1993 Don Arndt
1993 Eddie Finnegan
1993 Steve Loya
1994 Bert Smith
1994 Richard Willborn
1996 David Stanley Harvey
1997 H.T. Waller
2002 Bill Gatti
2000 Dennis Graser
2001 Rick (The Crusher) Scherr
2001 Don Clatterbough
2003 Ronnie Ford
2007 Mike Macenko

Men's Modified Pitch
1997 Frank Cecero
1998 Peter Ralph Miscione

Women's Fast-Pitch
1957 Amy Peralta Shelton
1957 Marie Wadlow
1959 Betty Evans Grayson
1960 Nina Korgan
1960 Ruth Sears

1963 Kay Rich
1964 Margaret Dobson
1965 Majorie Law
1966 Carolyn Thome Hart
1969 Jeanne Contel
1969 Micki Stratton
1970 Dot Wilkinson
1971 Virginia Busick
1972 Bertha Tickey
1973 Estelle (Ricki) Caito
1973 Gloria May
1975 Kathryn (Sis) King
1976 Pat Harrison
1976 Pat Walker
1980 Jean Daves
1981 Carol Spanks
1981 Shirley Topley
1982 Nancy Welborn
1982 Nance Ito
1982 Billie Harris
1983 Donna Lopiano
1983 Joan Joyce
1984 Jackie Rice
1985 Sharron Backus
1985 Willie Roze
1985 E. Louise Albrecht
1986 Chris Miner
1986 Peggy Kellers
1987 Lorene Ramsey
1987 Rose Marie Adams
1991 Marilyn Rau
1991 Marlys Taber Watts
1992 Diane Schumacher
1992 Carolyn Fitzwater
1995 Dorothy Dobie
1996 Kathy Arendsen
1997 Gina Vecchione
1998 Freda Savona
1999 Barbara Reinalda
2001 Suzie Gaw
2005 Pat Dufficy
2006 Sheila (Cornell) Douty

2006 Michele Granger
2006 Dot Richardson
2006 Michele Smith
2007 Louise Mazzuca
2008 Roberta (Robbie) Mulkey

Women's Slow-Pitch
1976 Alberta Kohls Sims
1978 Norma Eschenbrenner Ante
1979 Donna Wolfe
1982 Judy Hedgecock
1983 Ida Jean (Hoppy) Hopkins

1994 Carol Bemis
1994 Sherri Pickard
1994 Linda Polley
1999 Nancy Oldham
2007 Brenda Smith Foster
2008 Jenni Harp Oliver

APPENDIX C
NATIONAL CHAMPIONSHIP STATISTICS
MEN'S MAJOR FAST-PITCH

CHAMPIONSHIP RECORDS

National Champions

1933: J. L. Friedman Boosters, Chicago, IL

1934: Ke-Nash-A Motormakers, Kenosha, WI

1935: Crimson Coaches, Toledo, OH

1936: Kodak Park, Rochester, NY

1937: Briggs Manufacturing, Detroit, MI

1938: Pohler's Café, Cincinnati, OH

1939: Nick Carr's Boosters, Covington, KY

1940: Kodak Park, Rochester, NY

1941: Bendix Brakes, South Bend, IN

1942: Deep Rock Oilers, Tulsa, OK

1943: Hammer Field Raiders, Fresno, CA

1944: Hammer Field Raiders, Fresno, CA

1945: Fort Wayne Zollner Pistons,
    Fort Wayne, IN

1946: Fort Wayne Zollner Pistons,
    Fort Wayne, IN

1947: Fort Wayne Zollner Pistons,
    Fort Wayne, IN

1948: Briggs Beautyware, Detroit, MI

1949: Tip Top Tailors, Toronto, Canada

1950: Bombers, Clearwater, FL

1951: Dow Chemical, Midland, MI

1952: Briggs Beautyware, Detroit, MI

1953: Briggs Beautyware, Detroit, MI

1954: Bombers, Clearwater, FL

1955: Raybestos Cardinals, Stratford, CT

1956: Bombers, Clearwater, FL

1957: Bombers, Clearwater, FL

1958: Raybestos Cardinals, Stratford, CT

1959: Sealmasters, Aurora, IL

1960: Bombers, Clearwater, FL

1961: Sealmasters, Aurora, IL

1962: Bombers, Clearwater, FL

1963: Bombers, Clearwater, FL

1964: Burch Tool, Detroit, MI

1965: Sealmasters, Aurora, IL

1966: Bombers, Clearwater, FL

1967: Sealmasters, Aurora, IL

1968: Bombers, Clearwater, FL

1969: Raybestos Cardinals, Stratford, CT

1970: Raybestos Cardinals, Stratford, CT

1971: Welty Way, Cedar Rapids, IA

1972: Raybestos Cardinals, Stratford, CT

1973: Bombers, Clearwater, FL

1974: Guanella Brothers, Santa Rosa, CA

1975: Rising Sun Hotel, Reading, PA

1976: Raybestos Cardinals, Stratford, CT

1977: Billard Barbell, Reading, PA

1978: Billard Barbell, Reading, PA

1979: McArdle Pontiac Cadillac, Midland, MI

1980: Peterbilt Western, Seattle, WA

1981: Decatur ADM, Decatur, IL

1982: Peterbilt Western, Seattle, WA

1983: Franklin Cardinals, West Haven, CT

1984: Coors Kings, Merced, CA

1985: Pay 'n Pak, Seattle, WA

1986: Pay 'n Pak, Seattle, WA

1987: Pay 'n Pak, Seattle, WA

1988: TransAire, Elkhart, IN

135

1989: Penn Corp, Sioux City, IA

1990: Penn Corp, Sioux City, IA

1991: Guanella Brothers, Rohnert Park, CA

1992: National Health Care Discount,
Sioux City, IA

1993: National Health Care Discount,
Sioux City, IA

1994: Decatur Pride, Decatur, IL

1995: Decatur Pride, Decatur, IL

1996: All Car, Green Bay, WI

1997: Tampa Bay Smokers, Tampa, FL

1998: Meierhoffer-Fleeman, St. Joseph, MO

1999: Decatur Pride, Decatur, IL

2000: Meierhoffer-Fleeman, St. Joseph, MO

2001: Frontier Casino Players, St. Joseph, MO

2002: Frontier Casino Players, St. Joseph, MO

2003: The Farm Tavern, Madison, WI

2004: The Farm Tavern, Madison, WI

2005: Tampa Bay Smokers, Tampa Bay, FL

2006: Circle Tap, Denmark, WI

2007: Patsy's, New York, NY

Most National Championships

10: Bombers, Clearwater, FL

7: Raybestos-Franklin Cardinals, Stratford, CT

4: Sealmasters, Aurora, IL

4: Decatur Pride-ADM, Decatur, IL

4: Briggs Beautyware, Detroit, MI

**Most Consecutive National Championships
(same sponsor)**

3: Zollner Pistons, Fort Wayne, IN

3: Pay 'n Pak, Seattle, WA

**Most Consecutive National Championships
(different sponsor)**

3: Frontier Casino – Meierhoffer Fleeman,
St. Joseph, MO

Most Valuable Players

1955: John Hunter, Bombers,
Clearwater, FL

1956: Harvey Sterkel, Sealmasters,
Aurora, IL

1957: Herb Dudley, Bombers,
Clearwater, FL

1958: Max Trahan, McDonald Scots,
Lake Charles, LA

1959: Harvey Sterkel, Sealmasters,
Aurora, IL

1960: Bill Simoni, Delta Merchants,
Stockton, CA

1961: Bonnie Jones, Burch Grinders,
Detroit, MI

1962: Weldon Haney, Bombers,
Clearwater, FL

1963: Weldon Haney, Bombers,
Clearwater, FL

1964: Bonnie Jones, Burch Gage & Tool,
Detroit, MI

1965: Joe Lynch, Sealmasters,
Aurora, IL

1966: Abe Baker, Providence Local 57,
Providence, RI

1967: Rich Balswick, Falcons,
Mt. View, CA

1968: Weldon Haney, Bombers,
Clearwater, FL

1969: Roy Burlison, Falcons,
Mt. View, CA

1970: John Anquillare, Raybestos Cardinals,
Stratford, CT

1971: Ty Stofflet, Rising Sun Hotel,
Reading, PA

1972: Metro Szeryk, Raybestos Cardinals,
Stratford, CT

1973: Bob McClish, Scenic Gaslight Realty,
Springfield, MO

1974: Ty Stofflet, Rising Sun Hotel,
Reading, PA

1975: Ty Stofflet, Rising Sun Hotel,
Reading, PA

1976: Al Lewis, Raybestos Cardinals,
Stratford, CT

1977: Ty Stofflet, Billard Barbell,
Reading, PA

1978: TIE: Ty Stofflet, Billard Barbell, Reading, PA
and Ted Hicks, CMI, Springfield, MO

1979: Jeff Peck, McArdle Pontiac Cadillac,
Midland, MI

1980: Graham Arnold, Peterbilt Western,
Seattle, WA

1981: Dave Scott, Decatur ADM,
Decatur, IL

1982: Butch Batt, Peterbilt Western,
Seattle, WA

1983: John Anquillare, Franklin Cardinals,
West Haven, CT

1984: Chuck Hamilton, Coors Kings,
Merced, CA

1985: Steve Newell, Pay 'n Pak,
Seattle, WA

1986: Jimmy Carrithers, Pay 'n Pak,
Seattle, WA

1987: Bruce Beard, Pay 'n Pak,
Seattle, WA

1988: TIE: Peter Meredith, TransAire, Elkhart, IN, and
Mike Piechnik, The Farm Tavern, Madison, WI

1989: Bill Boyer, Penn Corp,
Sioux City, IA

1990: Mark Sorenson, Penn Corp,
Sioux City, IA

1991: Chubb Tangaroa, Guanella Brothers,
Rohnert Park, CA

1992: Mark Sorenson, National Health Care
Discount, Sioux City, IA

1993: Chubb Tangaroa, Decatur Pride,
Decatur, IL

1994: Rick Dohogne, Decatur Pride,
Decatur, IL

1995: Avon Meacham, Decatur Pride,
Decatur, IL

1996: Steve Schott, Tampa Bay Smokers,
Tampa Bay, FL

1997: Richard (Boomer) Brush, Tampa Bay Smokers,
Tampa Bay, FL

1998: Grover Musser, Meierhoffer-Fleeman,
St. Joseph, MO

1999: Shawn Rychcik, Decatur Pride,
Decatur, IL

2000: Kerry Shaw, Meierhoffer Fleeman,
St. Joseph, MO

2001: Kerry Shaw, St. Joseph Frontier Casino,
St. Joseph, MO

2002: Mike Dryer, St. Joseph Frontier Casino,
St. Joseph, MO

2003: Chris Delarwelle, The Farm Tavern,
Madison, WI

2004 : Dean Holoien, The Farm Tavern,
Madison, WI

2005: Adam LaLonde, Tampa Bay Smokers,
Tampa Bay, FL

2006 : Chris Delarwelle, The Farm Tavern,
Madison, WI

2007 : Zeron Winters, The Farm Tavern,
Madison, WI

Batting Champions

1950: Ed Tyranski, Briggs Beautyware,
Detroit, MI, .615

1951: John Zula, Chiefs,
Calumet City IL, .535

1952: Joe Overfield, Lackland, AFB,
San Antonio, TX .545

1953: Joe Morecraft, Trenton Democratic Club,
Baltimore, MD, .375

1954: Al Martin, Naval Air Station,
Denver, CO, .455

1955: Marion Cook, Standard Parts,
Memphis, TN, .500

1956: Bob Forbes, Bombers,
Clearwater, FL, .471

1957: Al McCoy, Norristown Blocks,
Norristown, PA, .467

1958: Domnick Golio, DeJur Camermen,
Long Island, NY, .421

1959: Clyde Miller, Champion YMCA,
Canton, NC, .500

1960: Frank Doucette, Merchants,
   Gardena, CA, .600
1961: LeRoy Hess, Sealmasters,
   Aurora, IL, .462
1962: Tom Moore, Bombers,
   Clearwater, FL, .444
1963: Joe Higgens, Mitchan Construction,
   Mesa, AZ, .455
1964: Ned Wickersham, Sealmasters,
   Aurora, IL, .438
1965: Ned Wickersham, Sealmasters,
   Aurora, IL, .500
1966: Ray Phillips, Fairchild Falcons,
   Mountain View, CA, .409
1967: Bill Parker, Bombers,
   Clearwater, FL, .409
1968: Weldon Haney, Bombers,
   Clearwater, FL, .412
1969: Charles Acklin, Armed Forces,
   Washington, D.C., .353
1970: John Anquillare, Raybestos Cardinals,
   Stratford, CT, .500
1971: Al Yeager, Raybestos Cardinals,
   Stratford, CT, .455
1972: Vince Caserto, Little Brahaus,
   Poughkeepsie, NY, .444
1973: Terry Muck, Whitaker Buick,
   St. Paul, MN, .467
1974: Bob Quinn, Home Savings & Loan,
   Aurora, IL, .467
1975: TIE: Larry Hale, Emerald Finance,
   Springfield, MO, and Abe Baker, Interstate
   Battery Men, Spencer, MA, .545
1976: Scott Simons, Sizzler Steak House,
   Salt Lake City, UT, .476
1977: George Bettineski, Peterbilt Western,
   Seattle, WA, .476
1978: Ted Hicks, CMI,
   Springfield, MO, .632
1979: Jim Brackin, Wilson Powell,
   Maryland Heights, MD, .533
1980: Bill Stewart, Peterbilt Western,

Seattle, WA, .524
1981: TIE: Leon Wood, Bombers,
   Clearwater, FL, and Steve Moore,
   Sunners, Reading, PA, .400
1982: Bruce Miller, Midland Explorers,
   Midland, MI, .417
1983: Jeff Seip, Sunners,
   Reading, PA, .500
1984: Jim Quick, The Farm Tavern,
   Madison, WI, .522
1985: Curt Peterson, Larry Miller Toyota,
   Salt Lake City, UT, .593
1986: Jim Brackin, Sunners,
   Reading, PA, .563
1987: Cleon Young, Midland Explorers,
   Midland, MI, .529
1988: Brian Rothrock, Decatur Pride,
   Decatur, IL, .458
1989: John Melchiori, Faultless Garber,
   Ashland, OH, .400
1990: Nick Genna, Guanella Brothers,
   Rohnert Park, CA, .538
1991: Dave Johnson, The Farm Tavern,
   Madison, WI, .500
1992: Jody Hennigar, Bombers,
   Clearwater, FL, .538
1993: Randy Peck, Heflin Builders,
   Middletown, NY, .500
1994: Mitch Munthe, SeaFirst Bank,
   Seattle, WA, .533
1995: Matt Kohnle, All Car,
   Green Bay, WI, .450
1996: Steve Schott, Smokers,
   Tampa, FL, .522
1997: Chris Delarwelle, The Farm Tavern,
   Madison, WI, .400
1998: Ross Dey, Meierhoffer Fleeman,
   St. Joseph, MO, .500
1999: Shawn Rychick, Decatur Pride,
   Decatur, IL, .533
2000: Brett Alvey, Larry Miller Toyota,
   Salt Lake City, UT, .538

2001: Trent Rubley, The Farm Tavern,
Madison, WI, .471

2002: TIE: Terry Boetsma, Midland Explorers,
Midland, MI, Mike Dryer, Frontier Casino
Players, St. Joseph, MO, and Blake Miller,
The Farm Tavern, Madison, WI, .500

2003: Dan Smet, The Farm Tavern,
Madison, WI, .615

2004: Tim Hatten, Blackhawk AC,
Rockford, IL, .667

2005: Adam LaLonde, Tampa Bay Smokers,
Tampa Bay, FL, .711 record

2006: Brad Johnson, Florida Fast-Pitch,
Jacksonville, FL, .586

2007: Thomas Makea, Patsy's,
New York, NY, .500

INDIVIDUAL PITCHING RECORDS

Most Strikeouts, Game

55: Herb Dudley, Bombers, Clearwater, FL
(1949) (21 innings)

46: Mike Piechnik, The Farm Tavern, Madison, WI
(1988) (20 innings)

40: Jim Chambers, Chicago Match Corporation,
Chicago, IL (1946) (19 innings)

38: Harry Kraft, Ke-Nash-A Motormakers,
Kenosha, WI (1934) (19 innings)

35: Roy Burlison, Anixter Brothers, Chicago, IL
(1971) (16 innings)

33: Ty Stofflet, Rising Sun Hotel, Reading, PA
(1971) (15 innings)

Most Strikeouts, Seven Inning Game

21: Dean Holoien, The Farm Tavern,
Madison, WI (2004)

20: Chris Wilson, Matarazzo Sea Dogs,
Stoneham, MA (1997)

19: John Hunter, Bombers,
Clearwater, FL (1950)

19: Harvey Sterkel, Sealmasters,
Aurora, IL (1959)

19: Richard Brubaker, Anxiter Bombers,
Skokie, IL (1971)

19: Chubb Tangaroa, Guanella Brothers,
Rohnert Park, CA (1991)

Most Consecutive Strikeouts, Game

20: Chubb Tangaroa, Decatur Pride,

Decatur, IL, (1993) (Fanned 28 of the 31
batters he faced and had a 1-0 no-hitter
through 10 innings)

Most Strikeouts by Two Pitchers, Game

81: Herb Dudley, Bombers, Clearwater, FL, and Arno
Lamb, Phillip's 66, Okmulgee, OK (1949)

75: Mike Piechnik, The Farm Tavern, Madison, WI,
and Peter Meredith, TransAire, Elkhart, IN (1988)

**Most Strikeouts by Two Pitchers Same Team,
Seven Inning Game**

20: Shifty Gears and Joe Witzigman, Kodak Park,
Rochester, NY (1936)

Most Strikeouts, Tournament

140: Mike Piechnik, The Farm Tavern,
Madison, WI (1988)

138: Peter Meredith, TransAire,
Elkhart, IN (1988)

130: Herb Dudley, Bombers,
Clearwater, FL (1949)

125: Darren Zack, SeaFirst Bank,
Seattle, WA (1992)

117: Jim Chambers, Chicago Match Corporation,
Chicago, IL (1946)

108: Harvey Sterkel, Sealmasters,
Aurora, IL (1960)

108: RoyBurlison, Fairchild Falcons,
Mt. View, CA (1969)

Most Innings Pitched, Tournament

88: Peter Meredith, TransAire,
    Elkhart, IN (1988)

77 2/3: Bonnie Jones, Burch Grinders,
    Detroit, MI (1961)

72 2/3: Chris Nicholas, Home Savings Loan,
    Aurora, IL (1984)

71: Mike Piechnik, The Farm Tavern,
    Madison, WI (1988)

71: Jim Chambers, Chicago Match Corporation,
    Chicago, IL (1946)

69: Herb Dudley, Bombers,
    Clearwater, FL (1949)

66: Roy Stephenson, Grumman Yankees,
    Long Island, NY (1951)

66: Bonnie Jones, Nothdurft Tool and Die,
    Detroit, MI (1970)

65 2/3: Harvey Sterkel, Sealmasters,
    Aurora, IL (1959)

62: Roy Burlison, Fairchild Falcons,
    Mt. View, CA (1969)

59: David Scott, Decatur ADM,
    Decatur, IL (1983)

58: Darren Zack, SeaFirst Bank,
    Seattle, WA (1992)

58: Bill Simoni, Delta Merchants,
    Stockton, CA (1960)

Most Games Pitched, Tournament

10: Bonnie Jones, Burch Grinders,
    Detroit, MI (1961)

9: Harvey Sterkel, Sealmasters,
    Aurora, IL (1959)

9: Darren Zack, SeaFirst Bank,
    Seattle, WA (1992)

9: Peter Meredith, TransAire,
    Elkhart, IN (1988)

Most Innings Without Allowing an Earned Run, Tournament

76 2/3 Ty Stofflet, Rising Sun Hotel,
    Reading, PA (1974–1975)

63: Mike Piechnik, The Farm Tavern,
    Madison, WI (1988)

55: Norb "Cyclone" Warken, Curlee Clothing,
    Covington, KY (1939)

50 2/3: Pete Meredith, TransAire,
    Elkhart, IN (1988)

Most Consecutive Scoreless Innings, Tournament

63: Mike Piechnik, The Farm Tavern,
    Madison, WI (1988)

Most Wins, Tournament

8: Peter Meredith, TransAire,
    Elkhart, IN (1988)

8: Graeme Robertson, Pay 'n Pak,
    Seattle, WA (1987)

8: Bonnie Jones, Burch Grinders,
    Detroit, MI (1961)

8: Harvey Sterkel, Sealmasters,
    Aurora, IL (1959)

7: Darren Zack, SeaFirst Bank,
    Seattle, WA (1992)

7: Roy Burlison, Fairchild Falcons,
    Mt. View, CA (1969)

Most Consecutive Wins, Tournament

14: Ty Stofflet, Rising Sun / York Barbell,
    Reading, PA (1977–1979)

13: Weldon Haney, Bombers,
    Clearwater, FL (1962–1965)

Most Hits Allowed, Tournament

42: Kevin Herlihy, Lancaster Chamelons,
    Lancaster, CA (1984)

38: Ty Stofflet, Sunners,
    Allentown, PA (1985)

Most Walks Allowed, Tournament

24: Gil Weslowski, Trenton Democratic Club,
    Baltimore, MD (1951)

INDIVIDUAL BATTING RECORDS

Highest Batting Average, Tournament

.711: Adam LaLonde, Tampa Bay Smokers,
Tampa Bay, FL (2005)

.667: Tim Haller, Blackhawk AC,
Rockford, IL (2004)

.632: Ted Hicks, CMI,
Springfield, MO (1978)

.615: Ed Tyranski, Briggs Beautyware,
Detroit, MI (1950)

.600: Frank Doucette, Merchants,
Gardena, CA (1960)

.593: Curt Peterson, Larry Miller Toyota,
Salt Lake City, UT (1985)

Highest Slugging Percentage, Tournament

1.583: Brad Johnson, Midwest GMC,
St. Louis, MO (1999)

1.538: Jody Hennigar, Bombers,
Clearwater, FL (1992)

1.471: Clayton McGovern, Midland Explorers,
Midland, MI (1999)

1.467: Shawn Rychick, Decatur Pride,
Decatur, IL (1999)

Most Hits, Game

4: Bob McClish, Scenic Gaslight Realty,
Springfield, MO (1973)

4: Ray Phillips, Fairchild Falcons,
Mt. View, CA (1966)

4: John Chestnut, Bombers,
Clearwater, FL (1949)

4: Art Upper, Tip Top Tailors,
Toronto, Canada (1949)

4: Shawn Rychcik, Decatur Pride,
Decatur, IL (1999)

4: Myron Guthrie, Bombers,
Clearwater, FL (1949)

4: Pete Turner, Nava Brothers,
Hayward, CA (1989)

4: Steve King, Hearts,
Bloomington, IL (1989)

4: Lonnie Swan, Aurora Lighting,
Aurora, IL (1993)

4: Steve Horning, Midland Explorers,
Midland, MI (2002)

4: Ehren Earlywine, Travelers,
St. Joseph, MO (1996)

4: Rich Lira, Meierhoffer,
St. Joseph, MO (2000)

Most Hits, Tournament

16: Curt Peterson, Larry Miller Toyota,
Salt Lake City, UT (1985)

14: Chuck Prescott, Sunners,
Reading, PA (1985)

13: Jack Johnson, Guanella Brothers,
Santa Rosa, CA (1985)

12: Ted Hicks, ADM, Decatur, IL (1983)

12: Don Van Deusen, Sunners,
Reading, PA (1983)

12: Scott Morris, Chameleons,
Lakewood, CA (1986)

12: Leon Wood, Bombers,
Clearwater, FL (1978)

12: Ted Hicks, CMI, Springfield, MO (1978)

12: Jim Quick, The Farm Tavern,
Madison, WI (1984)

12: Steve Schott, Smokers, Tampa, FL (1996)

11: Brian Rothrock, ADM, Decatur, IL (1983)

11: Steve Kerian, ADM, Decatur, IL (1983)

11: Glenn Beamon, LeBlanc Barons,
Sunnyvale, CA (1973)

11: Ricky Tomlinson, Bombers,
Clearwater, FL (1960)

11: Al Linde, Dow Chemical,
Midland, MI (1951)

11: Ray Allena, Guanella Brothers,
Santa Rosa, CA (1979)

11: Brian Rothrock, Decatur Pride,
Decatur, IL (1988)

Most Doubles, Tournament

5: George Bettineski, Peterbilt Western,
   Seattle, WA (1977)

5: Al Linde, Dow Chemical,
   Midland, MI (1951)

5: Steve Newell, Pay 'n Pak,
   Seattle, WA (1985)

5: Mike Parnow, Guanella Brothers,
   Rohnert Park, CA (1991)

Most Triples, Tournament

5: Jim Henley, Flames, Chattanooga, TN (1965)

4: John McEldowney, TransAire, Elkart, IN (1987)

3: Bill Massey, Raybestos Cardinals,
   Stratford, CT (1962)

Most Home Runs, Game

3: Jody Hennigar, Bombers, Clearwater, FL (1992)

3: Bob McClish, Scenic Gaslight Realty,
   Springfield, MO (1973)

Most Home Runs, Tournament

5: Clayton McGovern, Midland Explorers,
   Midland, MI (1999)

5: Bob McClish, Scenic Gaslight Realt,
   Springfield, MO (1973)

5: Jody Hennigar, The Farm Tavern,
   Madison, WI (1994)

4: Chris Delarwelle, Circle Tap,
   Denmark, WI (2003)

4: Todd Garcia, Team Lyons, Fresno, CA (2003)

4: George Krembel, Kodak Park,
   Rochester, NY (1935)

4: Jeff Seip, Sunners, Reading, PA (1985)

4: Bill Robeson, Deep Rock Oilers,
   Tulsa, OK (1942)

4: Bill Stewart, Peterbilt Western,
   Seattle, WA (1980)

4: Mark Sorenson, Penn Corp,
   Sioux City, IA (1993)

4: Steve Scott, Midland Explorers,
   Midland, MI (1991)

4: Randy Burnside, Penn Corp,
   Sioux City, IA (1991)

4: David Boys, Smokers, Tampa Bay, FL (1998)

4: Todd Schultz, Midland Explorers,
   Midland, MI (1999)

4: Shawn Rychick, Decatur Pride,
   Decatur, IL (1999)

Most Consecutive Games Hitting a Home Run

4: George Krembel, Kodak Park,
   Rochester, NY (1935)

Most RBIs, One Inning

7: Mitch Munthe, Larry Miller Toyota,
   Salt Lake City, UT (1997)

4: Chris Delarwelle, Circle Tap,
   Denmark, WI (2003)

Most RBIs, Game

8: Mitch Munthe, Larry Miller Toyota,
   Salt Lake City, UT (1997)

8: Brett Alvey, Larry Miller Toyota,
   Salt Lake City, UT (1997)

7: Bob McClish, Scenic Gaslight,
   Springfield, MO (1973)

6: Frank DeGroat, Patsy's New York City,
   New York, NY (2007)

6: Joe Morecraft, Trenton Democratic Club,
   Baltimore, MD (1953)

6: Chris Delarwelle, Circle Tap,
   Denmark, WI (2003)

6: Randy Brown, Vorco Products,
   Atlanta, GA (1984)

6: Mike Gomez, Stroh's, St. Paul, MN (1992)

6: Kerry Shaw, Meierhoffer,
   St. Joe, MO (2000)

5: Bobby Blakley, Bass Country Inn,
   Springfield, MO (1993)

5: Rick Hetherington, California Kings,
   Merced, CA (1985)

5: Rick Allen, Charlie's Trading Post,
   Atlanta, GA (1985)

5: Bob Clay, Sunners, Reading, PA (1985)

5: Shawn Rychick, Decatur Pride, Decatur, IL (1999)

5: Tommy Gray, Miller Toyota, Salt Lake City, UT (1999)

5: Bill Stewart, Peterbilt Western, Seattle, WA (1979)

5: Greg Melchert, Midland Explorers, Midland, MI (2000)

Most RBIs, Tournament

14: Shawn Rychcik, Decatur Pride, Decatur, IL (1999)

13: Bob McClish, Scenic Gaslight Realty, Springfield, MO (1973)

13: Chris Delarwelle, Circle Tap, Denmark, WI (2003)

13: Todd Garcia, Team Lyons, Fresno, CA (2003)

13: David Boys, Smokers, Tampa Bay, FL (1998)

12: Clayton McGovern, Midland Explorers, Midland, MI (1999)

12: Chuck Prescott, Sunners, Reading, PA (1985)

12: Brian Rothrock, ADM, Decatur, IL (1983)

10: Joe Molinaro, Little Brauhaus, Poughkeepsie, NY (1972)

10: Bill Wojie, Raybestos Cardinals, Stratford, CT (1956)

Most RBIs, Championship Game

5: Bill Wojie, Raybestos Cardinals, Stratford, CT (1956)

Most Runs Scored, Tournament

11: Pete Turner, Guanella Brothers, Rohnert Park, CA (1990)

10: Denny Place, Decatur Pride, Decatur, IL (1983)

10: Curt Peterson, Larry Miller Toyota, Salt Lake City, UT (1985)

Total Bases, Tournament

25: Jim Clark, Guanella Brothers, Santa Rosa, CA (1999)

24: Clayton McGovern, Midland Explorers, Midland, MI (1999)

24: Chris Delarwelle, Circle Tap, Denmark, WI (2003)

24: David Boys, Smokers, Tampa Bay, FL (1998)

20: Todd Schultz, Midland Explorers, Midland, MI (1999)

22: Shawn Rychick, Decatur Pride, Decatur, IL (1999)

22: Steve DeFrazio, Guanella Brothers, Santa Rosa, CA (1990)

21: Steve Schott, Smokers, Tampa Bay, FL (1996)

21: Marty Kernaghan, National Health Care Discount, Sioux City, IA (1992)

21: Todd Garcia, Team Lyons, Fresno, CA (2003)

20: Mark Sorenson, National Health Care Discount, Sioux City, IA (1993)

TEAM FIELDING RECORDS

Highest Fielding Percentage, Tournament

1.000: Raybestos Cardinals, Stratford, CT (1976)

.993: Miller All-Stars, Memphis, TN (1951)

Most Putouts, Game

93: Clearwater, FL Bombers and McKee Ramblers, Portland, PA (1963)

Most Putouts, Tournament

261: Penn Corp, Sioux City, IA (1991) and Guanella Brothers, Rohnert Park, CA (1990)

Most Assists, Game

32: Clearwater, FL Bombers (1963)

31: McKee Ramblers, Portland, OR (1963)

Most Assists, Tournament

98: Pay 'n Pak, Seattle, WA (1987)

Most Double Plays, Tournament

12: Clearwater, FL Bombers (1955)

Most Errors, Game

9: San Bernardino Lite All-Stars, San Bernardino, CA (1985)

Most Errors, Tournament

16: Allentown, PA Sunners (1985)

13: Steve's Flowers, Casper, Wyoming, and Georgian Enterprises, San Gabriel, CA (1958); State Farm Insurance, Bloomington, Illinois (1954)

12: Texas Gators, Lake Jackson, TX (1953); San Bernardino Lite All-Stars, San Bernardino, CA (1985).

TEAM BATTING RECORDS

Highest Batting Average, Tournament

.369: Decatur Pride, Decatur, IL (1999)

.345: California Kings, Merced, CA (1985)

.334: National Health Care Discount, Sioux City, IA (1992)

Most Hits, Game

23: Larry Miller Toyota, Salt Lake City, UT (1997)

20: Larry Miller Toyota, Salt Lake City, UT (1985)

Most Hits, Tournament

97: National Health Care Discount, Sioux City, IA (1992)

97: Guanella Brothers, Rohnert Park, CA (1990)

Most Home Runs, Game

5: The Farm Tavern, Madison, WI (2004)

Most Runs, Game

24: Miller Toyota, Salt Lake City, UT (1997)

Most Runs Scored, Tournament

73: Guanella Brothers, Rohnert Park, CA (1990)

Most Stolen Bases, Tournament

12: Topeka, KS, Capitols (1993)

9: National Health Care Discount, Sioux City, IA (1992)

9: Strategic Air Command, Offutt, AFB, NE (1966)

9: Decatur Pride, Decatur, IL (1996)

APPENDIX D
NATIONAL CHAMPIONSHIP STATISTICS
WOMEN'S MAJOR FAST-PITCH

National Champions

1933: Great Northern Laundry, Chicago, IL

1934: Hart Motors, Chicago, IL

1935: Weaver-Wall Bloomer Girls, Cleveland, OH

1936: National Screw and Manufacturing Co., Cleveland, OH

1937: National Screw and Manufacturing Co., Cleveland, OH

1938: J.J. Krieg's, Alameda, CA

1939: J.J. Krieg's, Alameda, CA

1940: Ramblers, Phoenix, AZ

1941: Higgins Midgets, Tulsa, OK

1942: Jax Maids, New Orleans, LA

1943: Jax Maids, New Orleans, LA

1944: Lind & Pomeroy, Portland, OR

1945: Jax Maids, New Orleans, LA

1946: Jax Maids, New Orleans, LA

1947: Jax Maids, New Orleans, LA

1948: Ramblers, Phoenix, AZ

1949: Ramblers, Phoenix, AZ

1950: Orange Lionettes, Orange, CA

1951: Orange Lionettes, Orange, CA

1952: Orange Lionettes, Orange, CA

1953: Betsy Ross Rockets, Fresno, CA

1954: Leach Motor Rockets, Fresno, CA

1955: Orange Lionettes, Orange, CA

1956: Orange Lionettes, Orange, CA

1957: Hacienda Rockets, Fresno, CA

1958: Raybestos Brakettes, Stratford, CT

1959: Raybestos Brakettes, Stratford, CT

1960: Raybestos Brakettes, Stratford, CT

1961: Gold Sox, Whittier, CA

1962: Orange Lionettes, Orange, CA

1963: Raybestos Brakettes, Stratford, CT

1964: Erv Lind Florists, Portland, OR

1965: Orange Lionettes, Orange, CA

1966: Raybestos Brakettes, Stratford, CT

1967: Raybestos Brakettes, Stratford, CT

1968: Raybestos Brakettes, Stratford, CT

1969: Orange Lionettes, Orange, CA

1970: Orange Lionettes, Orange, CA

1971: Raybestos Brakettes, Stratford, CT

1972: Raybestos Brakettes, Stratford, CT

1973: Raybestos Brakettes, Stratford, CT

1974: Raybestos Brakettes, Stratford, CT

1975: Raybestos Brakettes, Stratford, CT

1976: Raybestos Brakettes, Stratford, CT

1977: Raybestos Brakettes, Stratford, CT

1978: Raybestos Brakettes, Stratford, CT

1979: Sun City Saints, Sun City, AZ

1980: Raybestos Brakettes, Stratford, CT

1981: Orlando Rebels, Orlando, FL

1982: Raybestos Brakettes, Stratford, CT

1983: Raybestos Brakettes, Stratford, CT

1984: California Diamond Blazers, Los Angeles, CA

1985: Hi-Ho Brakettes, Stratford, CT

1986: Southern California Invasion, West Covina, CA

1987: Orange County Majestics,
    Orange County, CA
1988: Hi-Ho Brakettes, Stratford, CT
1989: Whittier Raiders, Whittier, CA
1990: Raybestos Brakettes, Stratford, CT
1991: Raybestos Brakettes, Stratford, CT
1992: Raybestos Brakettes, Stratford, CT
1993: Rebels, Redding, CA
1994: Rebels, Redding, CA
1995: Rebels, Redding, CA
1996: California Commotion, Woodland Hills, CA
1997: California Commotion, Woodland Hills, CA
1998: California Commotion, Woodland Hills, CA
1999: California Commotion, Woodland Hills, CA
2000: Storm, Phoenix, AZ
2001: Storm, Phoenix, AZ
2002: Stratford Brakettes, Stratford, CT
2003: Stratford Brakettes, Stratford, CT
2004: Stratford Brakettes, Stratford, CT
2005: Schutt Hurricanes, Lake Forest, CA
2006: Stratford Brakettes, Stratford, CT
2007: Stratford Brakettes, Stratford, CT

Most National Championships
28: Raybestos Brakettes, Stratford, CT
8: Orange Lionettes, Orange, CA
5: Jax Maids, New Orleans, LA
4: Commotion, Woodland Hills, CA

Most Consecutive National Championships
8: Raybestos Brakettes, Stratford, CT
    (1971–1978)

Most Valuable Players
1950: Bertha Ragan, Orange County Lionettes,
    Orange, CA
1951: Bertha Ragan, Orange County Lionettes,
    Orange, CA
1952: Bertha Ragan, Orange County Lionettes,
    Orange, CA
1953: Bertha Ragan, Orange County Lionettes,
    Orange, CA

1954: Kay Rich, Leach Motor Rockets,
    Fresno, CA
1955: Bertha Ragan, Orange County Lionettes,
    Orange, CA
1956: Bertha Ragan, Raybestos Brakettes,
    Stratford, CT
1957: Virginia Busick, Hacienda Rockets,
    Fresno, CA
1958: Bertha Ragan, Raybestos Brakettes,
    Stratford, CT
1959: Bertha Ragan, Raybestos Brakettes,
    Stratford, CT
1960: Bertha Ragan, Raybestos Brakettes.
    Stratford, CT
1961: Joan Joyce, Raybestos Brakettes,
    Stratford, CT
1962: Louise Albrecht, Whittier Gold Sox,
    Whittier, CA
1963: Joan Joyce, Raybestos Brakettes,
    Stratford, CT
1964: Jackie Rice, Erv Lind Florists,
    Portland, OR
1965: Joan Joyce, Orange County Lionettes,
    Orange, CA
1966: Donna Lopiano, Raybestos Brakettes,
    Stratford, CT
1967: Mary Miller, OHSE Meats,
    Topeka, KS
1968: Joan Joyce, Raybestos Brakettes,
    Stratford, CT
1969: Billie Harris, Yakima Webb Cats,
    Yakima, WA
1970: Nancy Welborn, Orange County Lionettes,
    Orange, CA
1971: Joan Joyce and Donna Lopiano,
    Raybestos Brakettes, Stratford, CT
1972: Donna Lopiano, Raybestos Brakettes,
    Stratford, CT
1973: Joan Joyce, Raybestos Brakettes,
    Stratford, CT
1974: Joan Joyce, Raybestos Brakettes,
    Stratford, CT

1975: Joan Joyce, Raybestos Brakettes,
Stratford, CT

1976: Barbara Reinalda, Raybestos Brakettes,
Stratford, CT

1977: Barbara Reinalda, Raybestos Brakettes,
Stratford, CT

1978: Diane Schumacher, Raybestos Brakettes,
Stratford, CT

1979: Marilyn Rau, Sun City Saints,
Sun City, AZ

1980: Debbie Doom, Sun City Saints,
Sun City, AZ

1981: Dot Richardson, Rebels,
Orlando, FL

1982: Michele Thomas, Sun City Saints,
Sun City, AZ

1983: Pat Dufficy, Raybestos Brakettes,
Stratford, CT

1984: Sue Lewis, LA Diamonds,
Los Angeles, CA

1985: Allison Rioux, Raybestos Brakettes,
Stratford, CT

1986: Liz Mizera, California Invasion,
Los Angeles, CA

1987: Michele Granger, Orange County Majestics,
Orange County, CA

1988: Michele Granger, Orange County Majestics,
Orange County, CA

1989: Dot Richardson, Hi-Ho Brakettes,
Stratford, CT

1990: Dot Richardson, Hi-Ho Brakettes,
Stratford, CT

1991: Lisa Fernandez, Raybestos Brakettes,
Stratford, CT

1992: Lisa Fernandez, Raybestos Brakettes,
Stratford, CT

1993: Michele Smith, Redding Rebels,
Redding, CA

1994: Kim Maher, Redding Rebels,
Redding, CA

1995: Michele Smith, Redding Rebels,
Redding, CA

1996: Dot Richardson, California Commotion,
Woodland Hills, CA

1997: Lisa Fernandez, California Commotion,
Woodland Hills CA

1998: Lisa Fernandez, California Commotion,
Woodland Hills, CA

1999: Lisa Fernandez, California Commotion,
Woodland Hills, CA

2000: Keira Goerl, Phoenix Storm,
Phoenix, AZ

2001: Keira Goerl, Phoenix Storm,
Phoenix, AZ

2002: Cat Osterman, Stratford Brakettes,
Stratford, CT

2003: Kelly Kretschman, Stratford Brakettes,
Stratford, CT

2004: Michelle Green, Stratford Brakettes,
Stratford, CT

2005: Ashley Herrera, Schutt Hurricanes,
Burbank, CA

2006: Candice Baker, Stratford Brakettes,
Stratford, CT

2007: Courtney Burnes, Stratford Brakettes,
Stratford, CA

Batting Champions

1950: Margaret Dobson, Erv Lind Florists,
Portland, OR,.615

1951: Mary Gilpin, Schrader Company,
Cleveland, OH, .545

1952: Loretta Chushuk, Kansas City Dons,
Kansas City, KS, .500

1953: Mary Baker, Canada Legion, Regina,
Canada,500

1954: Marge Grant, Cannerettes,
Olympia, WA, .500

1955: Kay Rich, Rockets,
Fresno, CA, .611

1956: Chick Long, Pennsylvania Girls,
Lancaster, PA, .600

1957: Delores Price, Erv Lind Florists,
Portland, Oregon, .416

1958: Jo Day, Orange County Lionettes,
Orange, CA, .467

1959: Eleanor Rudolph, Pekin Lettes,
Pekin, IL . 454

1960: Dot Wilkinson, Ramblers,
Phoenix, AZ, .444

1961: Pam Kurrell, Lock Drug Jets,
Redwood City, CA . 571

1962: Janet Dicks, Crystal-ettes,
Reading, PA, .429

1963: Carol Lee, Whittier Gold Sox,
Whittier, CA, .438

1964: Joy Peterson, Shamrocks,
Salt Lake City UT, .545

1965: Jan Berkland, Comets,
Minneapolis, MN . 455

1966: Edwina Bryan, Lorelei Ladies,
Atlanta, GA,.571

1967: Jane Hughes, Shamrocks,
Salt Lake City, UT, .471

1968: Toni Swartout, Rebels,
Orlando, FL, .500

1969: Carol Lichtenberger, Schaeferettes,
Plainfield, NJ, .600

1970: Cathy Benedetto, Dr. Bernard's,
Portland, OR, .412

1971: Joan Joyce, Raybestos Brakettes,
Stratford, CT,.429

1972: Donna Lopiano, Raybestos Brakettes,
Stratford, CT., 429

1973: Judy Jungwirth, Benjos,
Bloomington, MN, .438

1974: Diane Kalliam, Santa Clara Laurels,
Santa Clara, CA ., 444

1975: Diane Kalliam, Santa Clara Laurels,
Santa Clara, CA, .632

1976: Barbara Reinalda, Raybestos Brakettes,
Stratford, CT, .450

1977: Cathy Toppi, Co-eds, Bridgeport, CT, .571

1978: Reathe Stucky, Arrows, Wichita, KS,
and Pam Reinoehl, Golden Bobcats,
Santa Clara, CA, .533

1979: Cindy Anderson, Bankettes,
West Allis, WI, .500

1980: Marilyn Rau, Sun City Saints,
Sun City, AZ, .520

1981: Pat Cutright, Macomb, Magic,
Macomb, Ill., 391

1982: Venus Jennings, Budweiser Belles,
Parsippany, NJ, .533

1983: Pat Guenzler, Raybestos Brakettes,
Stratford, CT, .563

1984: Sue Lewis, LA Diamonds,
Los Angeles, CA, .421

1985: Barb Drake, Sitton Transportation,
Jefferson City, MO, .500

1986: Liz Mizera, Invasion,
Hacienda Heights, CA, .350

1987: Kari Johnson, Redding Rebels,
Redding, CA, .476

1988: Gina Vecchione, Raybestos Brakettes,
Stratford, CT, .444

1989: Dot Richardson, Hi-Ho Brakettes,
Stratford, CT, .393

1990: Chenita Rogers, California Invasion,
Walnut, CA. 450

1991: Charlotte Wiley, California Knights,
Burbank, CA, .542

1992: Janice Parks, California Commotion,
Diamond Bar, CA .500

1993: Kathy Kreischer, Topton VIPs,
Topton, PA, .456

1994: Cathy Wylie, Redding Rebels,
Redding, CA,.471

1995: Dionna Harris, Southern California Jazz,
San Gabriel, CA, .611

1996: Kim Maher, Redding Rebels,
Redding, CA, .500

1997: Cindy Smith, Phoenix Sunbirds,
Phoenix, AZ, .534

1998: Danielle Cox, Twister,
Decatur, IL, .688 (record)

1999: Lisa Fernandez, California Commotion,
Woodland Hills, CA, .556

2000: Jen Stump, Sun Sox,
 Winter Garden, FL, .429

2001: Veronica Marmatt, East Peoria Avanti's,
 East Peoria, Il, .571

2002: Liz Dennis, Iowa Dynasty,
 Iowa City, IA, .476

2003: Lyndsey Angus, Storm USA,
 Lake Forest, CA, .556

 2004: Danielle Kaminka, Schutt Hurricanes,

Burbank, CA and Courtney Fossatti,
 Schutt Hurricanes, Burbank, CA, .476

2005: Kristine Rochette, Connecticut Classics,
 New Haven, CT, . 500

2006: Kaitlin Cochran, Southern California Sliders,
 Yorba Linda, CA, .533

2007: Sarah Clynes, Carbondale Cougars,
 Carbondale, Ill., .600

INDIVIDUAL PITCHING RECORDS

Most Strikeouts, Game

40: Joan Joyce, Raybestos Brakettes, Stratford, CT
 (19 innings) (1961)

33: Tiffany Boyd, California Raiders,
 Santa Monica, CA (27 innings) (1987)

32: Becky Duffin, Pantera's Classic,
 Jefferson City, MO (27 innings) (1987)

32: Leslie Partch, Bettencourt Blast, Hayward, CA
 (17 innings) (1984)

Most Strikeouts, Seven Inning Game

20: Bertha Tickey, Orange Lionettes,
 Orange, CA (1953)

20: Michele Granger, Orange County Majestics,
 Orange County, CA (1988)

19: Bertha Tickey, Orange Lionettes,
 Orange, CA (1954)

Most Consecutive Strikeouts, Game

18: Michele Granger, Orange County Majestics,
 Orange County, CA (1988)

16: Louise Mazzuca, Erv Lind Florists,
 Portland, OR (1959)

16: Michele Granger, Orange County Majestics,
 Orange County, CA (1988)

11: Bertha Tickey, Raybestos Brakettes,
 Stratford, CT (1968)

Most Strikeouts by Two Pitchers, Game

65: Becky Duffin, Pantera's Classic, Jefferson City,
 MO, and Tiffany Boyd, California Raiders, Santa
 Monica, CA (1987)

Most Strikeouts, Tournament

134: Joan Joyce, Raybestos Brakettes,
 Stratford, CT (1973)

Most Innings Pitched, Tournament

70: Joan Joyce, Raybestos Brakettes,
 Stratford, CT (1973)

69 2/3: Joan Joyce, Raybestos Brakettes,
 Stratford, CT (1974)

Most No-Hitters, National Tournament

3: Louise Mazzuca, Erv Lind Florists,
 Portland, OR (1960)

Most Perfect Games, Tournament

2: Bertha Tickey, Raybestos Brakettes,
 Stratford, CT (1950 and 1954)

2: Margie Law, Ramblers, Phoenix, AZ
 (1954 and 1957)

Most Wins, Tournament

8: Joan Joyce, Raybestos Brakettes,
 Stratford, CT (1973)

7: Joan Joyce, Raybestos Brakettes,
 Stratford, CT (1974)

INDIVIDUAL BATTING RECORDS

Highest Batting Average, Tournament

.688: Danielle Cox, Twister, Decatur, IL (1998)

.632: Diane Kalliam, Laurels,
Santa Clara, CA (1975)

Most Hits, Game

5: Kay Rich, Rockets, Fresno, CA (1955)

5: Tricia Popowski, Raybestos Brakettes,
Stratford, CT (1992)

Most Hits, Tournament

16: Pat Guenzler, Raybestos Brakettes,
Stratford, CT (1983)

Most Consecutive Hits, Tournament

9: Kris Peterson, Raybestos Brakettes,
Stratford, CT (1987)

Most Doubles, Tournament

6: Dot Richardson, Raybestos Brakettes,
Stratford, CT (1989)

Most Triples, Tournament

3: Irene Huber, Rockets, Fresno, CA (1949)

3: Marilyn Rau, Sun City Saints,
Sun City, AZ (1978 and 1981)

3: Lu Flanagan, Jolos, Seattle, WA (1971)

3: Lana Svec, Sarver Paving,
Ashland, OH (1977)

Most Home Runs, Tournament

5: Kim Maher, Rebels, Redding, CA (1994)

4: Robbie Mulkey, Erv Lind Florists,
Portland, OR (1949)

Most Runs Scored, Tournament

12: Willie Roze, Raybestos Brakettes,
Stratford, CT (1975)

9: Kris Peterson, Raybestos Brakettes,
Stratford, CT (1987)

9: Pat Dufficy, Raybestos Brakettes,
Stratford CT (1983)

9: Irene Shea, Raybestos Brakettes,
Stratford, CT (1975)

9: Micki Stratton, Raybestos Brakettes,
Stratford, CT (1965)

Most RBIs, Game

7: Dionna Harris, Raybestos Brakettes,
Stratford, CT (1992)

6: Joan Joyce, Raybestos Brakettes,
Stratford, CT (1975)

6: Kay Rich, Hacienda Rockets,
Fresno, CA (1955)

Most RBIs, Tournament

12: Kim Maher, Rebels, Redding, CA (1994)

10: Pat Dufficy, Raybestos Brakettes,
Stratford, CT (1983)

10: Kay Rich, Hacienda Rockets,
Fresno, CA (1955)

Most At-Bats, National Championship

42: Jackie Gaw, Raybestos Brakettes,
Stratford, CT (1983)

42: Irene Shea, Raybestos Brakettes,
Stratford, CT (1974)

TEAM FIELDING RECORDS

Highest Fielding Percentage, Tournament

.996: Raybestos Brakettes, Stratford, CT (1965)

.994: Raybestos Brakettes, Stratford, CT (1959)

Most Putouts, Game

81: California Raiders, Santa Monica, CA and
    Pantera's Classic, Jefferson City, MO (1987)

Most Putouts, Tournament

277: Raybestos Brakettes, Stratford, CT (1961)

Most Assists, Tournament

124: Raybestos Brakettes, Stratford, CT (1983)

Most Double Plays, Tournament

7: Erv Lind Florists Portland, OR (1949)

5: Rockets, Fresno, CA (1963)

5: Burry Biscuit, Plainfield, NJ (1960)

TEAM BATTING RECORDS

Highest Batting Average, Tournament

.358: Raybestos Brakettes, Stratford, CT (1983)

Most Hits, Game

27: Raybestos Brakettes, Stratford, CT (1992)

Most Hits, Tournament

118: Raybestos Brakettes, Stratford, CT (1983)

Most Doubles, Tournament

12: Raybestos Brakettes, Stratford, CT
    (1968 and 1983)

Most Triples, Tournament

7: Ramblers, Phoenix, AZ (1955)

7: Sarver Paving, Ashland, OH (1977)

Most Home Runs, Tournament

10: Raybestos Brakettes, Stratford, CT (1992)

Most Runs Scored, Inning

12: Raybestos Brakettes, Stratford, CT (1992)

Most Runs Scored, Game

30: Raybestos Brakettes, Stratford, CT (1992)

Most Runs Scored, Tournament

58: Raybestos Brakettes, Stratford, CT
    (1957, 1983, and 1992)

Most RBIs, Game

26: Raybestos Brakettes, Stratford, CT (1992)

Most Stolen Bases, Tournament

14: Erv Lind Florists, Portland, OR (1962)

MISCELLANEOUS RECORDS

Most Games Played, Tournament

11: Raybestos Brakettes, Stratford, CT (1983)

Most Wins Coming Out of Losers' Bracket

9: Raybestos Brakettes, Stratford, CT (1983)

BIBLIOGRAPHY

Babb, Ron. *Etched in Gold*. Indianapolis, IN: Masters Press, 1997.

Beale, Morris A. *The Softball Story*. Washington, DC: Columbia Publishing Company, 1957.

Canarelli, Louis. "Canarelli Hails Progress of 53 Urges Drive Toward New Goals." *Balls and Strikes*. February 1954: p. 3.

Crosby, Fred D. "Opportunities Ahead for Softball in '60's." *Balls and Strikes*. February 1960: p. 4.

Deaver, John W. "ASA 25th Anniversary Stirs March of Time Recollections." *Balls and Strikes*. August 1957: p. 1, 8.

Dickson, Paul. *The Worth Book of Softball*. New York: Facts on File, 1994.

Dobbs, Lou. *Independents Day: Awakening the American Spirit*. New York: Viking Penguin, 2007.

Friedman, Milton and Schwartz, Anna Jacobson. *A Monetary History of the United States*. New Jersey: Princeton University Press, 1963.

Feigner, Eddie, Feigner, Anne Marie, Lyons Douglas, B. *From an Orphan to a King*. Wayne, MI: Immortal Investments Publishing, 2004.

Fischer, Leo H. *How to Play Winning Softball*. New York: Prentice-Hall, Inc. 1940.

Fulton, John W. "Nation's Leading Sport?—Softball by Far." *Balls and Strikes*. May 1954: p. 1.

Johnson, Raymond. "Thoughts of an X President." *Balls and Strikes*. December-January 1948: pp. 1, 4.

Keady, Jack. "Softball Still King with Otto Smith." *Arkansas Democrat*. March 1957: p. 4.

Klein, Willie. "Ragan Tells TV Audience of Hill Feats." *Balls and Strikes*. December 1954: p. 8.

Klein, Willie. "Canarelli Gets Post as Prexy." *Balls and Strikes*. February 1953: pp. 1, 7.

Klein, Willie. "Umps Converge on N.Y. for First National Clinic." *Balls and Strikes*. March 1953: pp. 1, 3.

Klein, Willie. "Believe It or Not Hails Bertha Ragan." *Balls and Strikes*. July 1954: p. 1.

Klein, Willie. "Crosby New ASA Prexy; 3 New VPs." *Balls and Strikes*. February 1960: pp. 1-5.

Klein, Willie. "ASA Appoints Special Committee to Study Youth Softball and Plan Guidance Program." *Balls and Strikes*. February 1956: p. 2.

Klein, Willie. "East-West All-Star Game Proposed by Raybestos." *Balls and Strikes*. February 1956: p. 5.

Klein, Willie. "Low-cost Group Insurance Plan Made Available to ASA members." *Balls and Strikes*. March 1957: p. 3.

Klein, Willie. "Silver-jacketed Guides Receive Compliments as Best Production Yet." *Balls and Strikes*. March 1957: p. 3.

Klein, Willie. "Recreational Progress Crosby's Life Work." *Balls and Strikes*. February 1960: p. 2.

Klein, Willie. "Stars Dot Lineups in East Major." *Balls and Strikes*. May 1960: pp. 1, 6.

Klein, Willie. "Porter Appointed Executive Sec'y-Treasurer." *Balls and Strikes*. February 1963: pp. 1, 4.

Landis, W. E. "Ballgames for Bendix." *Softballers Magazine*. April-May 1938: pp. 8-10, 28-29.

Littlewood, Mary L. *The Path to the Gold–An Historical Look at Women's Fastpitch in the United States*. Columbia, MO: NFCA, 1998.

Mason, Tom. *Life's Journey in Different Uniforms*. New Castle, DE: Associated Graphics System, 2000.

Martin, B.E. "Greatest Show on Earth? Ask the Thousands Who Attended Women's World Play in Orange." *Balls and Strikes*. September 1954: pp. 2, 8.

Martin, B.E. "Softball Earns Increasing Attention." *Balls and Strikes*. February 1960: p. 2.

Nelson, Roger. *The Zollner Piston Story*. Fort Wayne, IN: The Allen County Public Library Foundation, 1995.

Pauley, M. J. "Elect Hakanson ASA President." *Balls and Strikes*. December-January 1948: pp. 1, 4.

Pauley, M. J. "Hakanson Appoints Committees." *Balls and Strikes*. February-March 1948: pp. 1, 4.

Pauley, M. J. "First Birthday of *Balls and Strikes*." *Balls and Strikes*. April 1948: p. 1.

Pauley, M. J. "*Balls and Strikes* Editorial." *Balls and Strikes*. August 1948: p. 2.

Plummer, Bill. "Softball's Centennial Celebration." *Balls and Strikes*. March 1987: pp. 3, 14.

Spencer, Bob. *A History of Kentucky Fastpitch Champions, 1935 Thru 1978*. Waddy, KY: 1979.

Whitmore, Seth. "Rule Changes Hit Pitcher." *Softball*. October 1939: pp. 1, 4.

Whitmore, Seth. "Ninety-six Championship Teams in Tournament." *Softball*. September 1940: p. 1.

ABOUT THE AUTHOR

Bill Plummer III is currently the ASA Hall of Fame Manager, editor of *The Inside Pitch*, and Trade Show Manager. Bill has received numerous awards for his sports writing and exceptional contributions to the sport of softball during his forty years of involvement in the ASA. An ASA Hall-of-Famer himself (1999, Meritorious Service), Bill served as an ASA umpire for fifteen years and is a former player and

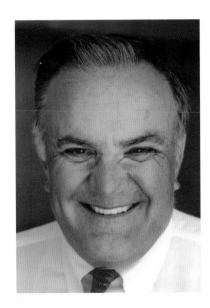

manager. A former deputy state commissioner and publicity director for the New York State ASA, Plummer joined the ASA National office in Oklahoma City in 1979, and for eighteen years has served as the Public Relations and Media Director. Bill is also the ASA's official historian. He lives in Oklahoma City, Oklahoma, and is a 1973 graduate of Indiana University, Bloomington, Indiana.

IMAGE CREDITS

TRADEMARKS

INDEX